**Praise for *Boscology***

*At the heart and core of every human being is the need to be seen, to be heard, and to be loved. These needs are part of the human DNA that ties us all together. Some leaders can satisfy one or more of these human needs when serving others. However, It is very rare for a leader to have this complete skillset for everyone they meet. It requires enormous patience, care, and love to be available and present for every person. Love is how we know we are seen, and how we know we are heard. There is no one who better represents this love for humanity than Dr. Pat Bosco. I have witnessed personally his rare humanity. He authentically makes every one feel they are the most important person in the world. Kansas State University is a better learning institution because of Dr. Pat Bosco—and the world is a better place because of this man.*

—Dr. Bernard Franklin, Ph.D.
Vice President of Student Life
Mount St. Mary's University

*Pat Bosco is the embodiment of what it means to be a 'K-Stater.' For over fifty years, he has been caring, selfless and tireless in his devotion to our university and its students.*

—Mary L. Vanier,
Kansas State University Foundation and
Mary L. Vanier K-State Family Scholarship

*Boscology is more than a self-help book on effective leadership. It is a primer on how to fully live, realizing potential, connecting with others and enjoying the process. Pat is an amazing man to know, he has boundless energy, is a joy to all he meets, AND was extremely adept at positively moving and effecting both individuals and organizations. He knows no stranger, only new friends with whom he connected and then connected with others. It made me wonder, how does he do it? We are now fortunate, for in this playbook he reveals his methods and magic.*

—Terry Matlack,
Founder and Managing Director of VantEdge Partners
and K-State College of Business Administration
Alumni Fellow

# BOSCOLOGY 101

## THE ART OF
## AUTHENTIC LEADERSHIP

**Pat J. Bosco, Ph.D.**

*Boscology 101*
Copyright©2020 by Pat J. Bosco, Ph.D.
All rights reserved

No part of this publication may reproduced or transferred in any manner or form, or by any means, electronic or mechanical except for brief parts for review purposes without the expressed written permission from the author or publisher.

Cataloging in Publication Data
Bosco, Pat J.
   Boscology 101
   .p cm.

ISBN 978-1-7352249-1-6

PCN
GV 844 B66 2020
658.4092 Bo

   1. Leadership Skills 2. Life Skills 3. Values
   4. Conduct of Life 5. Authentic Life

Cover photo: Evert Nelson of the K-State Royal Purple

Back cover photo: Logan Wassall of the Collegian Media Group

Printed in the United States of America

## DEDICATION

*To my students and their families
and for those who put them first.*

**TABLE OF CONTENTS**

Foreword *by Susan Edgerley 9*

Introduction *13*

Top Twenty Life Notions *15*

Leadership   17
    Servant Leadership *19*
    The Characteristics of Authentic Leadership *25*
    The Art of Authentic Leadership *29*
    Transparency *32*

Teams *37*
    Effective Teams are Winning Teams *38*
    Effective Followers *41*
    Creating a Welcoming Environment *44*
    Delegating *52*

Communication *58*
    The Power of Listening *60*
    Communication *68*
    The First Question Should be "Why?" *73*
    First Impressions *77*

Giving Service to Others *80*
    Respect *82*
    Taking the Initiative *85*
    Paying the Debt *88*
    Thanking Your Heroes *91*

Setting Goals *94*
    Goal Setting *96*
    Attention to Detail *101*
    What Ifs *104*
    Be Open to Change *111*

Success *115*
    Defining Success *117*
    Discipline is Key to Success *121*
    Nobody's Perfect *124*
    Legacy: What's Next? *127*

About the Author *131*

Acknowledgements *135*

## FOREWORD

*By Susan Edgerley*

In my almost 30 years as an editor at *The New York Times,* I would tell aspiring editors that to be a good leader, people have to want to follow you. I would tell them it's not about the crown they put on your head; it's the crown you earn. Pat Bosco is that kind of leader, wearing that kind of crown.

That teacher, or coach, or camp counselor you'll never forget—that's my friend Pat. I met him 45 years ago when he was an Assistant Dean at just 24, and was directing student services and the advisor to several student organizations at Kansas State University.

Pat has been a mentor and role model to thousands of students in his 50-plus years at K-State. He is a commonsensical sage, wise to the secret of a life well lived, long before the concepts of mindfulness and gratitude exploded in popular culture.

Pat was showing us the way to live as a graduate student in the 1970s, and he showed so many others in the decades that followed, listening and helping as he climbed the ranks at his land-grant school in Manhattan, Kansas—a place everyone calls "The Little Apple."

I remember Pat running up and down the bleachers of the football stadium with boxes of doughnuts in his arms, handing them out to students who were waiting in the cold to buy season tickets. I remember him waving from his window in Anderson Hall to students walking to class. I remember looking up at that window as an adult not so long ago, hoping he would see me on the sidewalk and wave.

Each year at freshman orientation, he would give his home phone number to the parents of every incoming student. He didn't stop paying attention when students graduated, or if they flunked out, or when he retired.

Pat looks and acts like a joyous Al Pacino, if you can imagine Pacino as a Vice President for student life at a state university in the Midwest. When my husband and kids met him, maybe 10 years ago, the rapport was instant. My oldest, Jack, wanted Pat to run for governor.

Leadership comes naturally to him. It is integral to his personality and his heart. He seems to have come to understand more easily than the rest of us that it's more rewarding—and frankly, easier—to be a good guy than a bad guy. He is inclusive, honorable, optimistic. It's a killer combination.

When Pat left K-State at the end of the 2018-19 academic year, he told me he wanted to do a podcast or write a book. I said I wanted to help. Because I love him, of course, and mostly, because he has so much to say, and I knew that others could benefit from his wisdom.

As I write these words during the COVID-19 pandemic and the Black Lives Matter movement, just a few days before the Fourth of July 2020, so much of Pat's wisdom feels like the beginnings of an antidote to our national illness: the divisiveness, the meanness, the tribal cruelty and lack of caring for one another. It is people like Pat who know how to turn it all around.

Take a look the Table of Contents. You'll see a section on servant leadership. Another on authentic leadership. Sections on listening, creating a welcoming environment, and thanking your heroes. Pat's lessons are a balm for our troubled souls.

## INTRODUCTION

I'VE SPENT OVER FIFTY YEARS as a student-life administrator at Kansas State University. My tenure at K-State grew over time from Student Body President to Director of Student Activities to Vice President for Student Life and Dean of Students. My entire professional career has been focused on helping students realize their potential. I have had the honor to interact with students, and their families, from every walk of life and from all over the United States and the world.

The purpose of this book is to encapsulate the half-century of practical lessons and perspective I have shared with students, which they call "Boscology." The original format for these dispatches is a podcast called *Boscology 101*. It is my hope that this book provides readers with a framework of how best to improve interactions with others at home, in school, or in the workplace, on and off the playing field—anyplace we can make a positive, lasting contribution and help ourselves and others be successful.

How success is defined is an individual choice and applies to many aspects of our lives, including work, family, and community. No matter how you define it, success requires a commitment to being authentic in all your interactions so you can grow into being an authentic leader.

Authentic leadership is rooted in a fundamental commitment to serving others and providing a voice to those who have none or have been silenced. Authentic leaders create healthy environments that promote consensus and a sense of belonging to something bigger than oneself. Authentic leadership is more than a phrase, and those willing to embrace it should be encouraged, celebrated, and nurtured so that it can be replicated in others. Real enthusiasm and passion can be cultivated, resulting in authenticity.

The various skill sets shared in this book include the importance of authenticity, sincerity, respect, caring, listening, welcoming, and being of service to others. Developing these skills is much like developing muscles or learning a musical instrument. It requires practice and repetition to be authentic. It also requires that we be open to change and input from others.

I recently retired from Kansas State University, but my interactions have not diminished. I still have the opportunity to practice these skills and share them with others. I am grateful for the lessons I continue to learn from others and am appreciative that you have given me the opportunity to share with you my own *Boscology*.

## TOP TWENTY LIFE NOTIONS

1. Always save room for dessert

2. Character is defined by what you do when no one else is looking

3. Do NOT hate

4. Define your own success

5. Admit your mistakes

6. Promise Little & Deliver Big

7. Show respect

8. Share credit

9. Do the very best job you can, no matter the task

10. When you *least* feel like it, do something nice for someone else

11. Do not be afraid to say: "I don't know." "I apologize." "Thank you." "Please." "I love you."

12. Ask good questions—especially "Why?"—and listen to the answers

13. Thank your heroes. Be someone else's hero.

14. Lose and win with class

15. Ask yourself often, "What can I do to help others function more effectively in my job, family, and community?"

16. When meeting a new person, introduce yourself with a smile

17. Teams are only as strong as their weakest player

18. Think before you write or say something stupid

19. Pray every day and include someone else in your prayers

20. How we deal with failures will define us more as human beings than our successes

## LEADERSHIP

BEING A LEADER requires more than just being in charge. Leadership comes with great responsibility and a desire to serve others. Before you can take on the role of a leader, you have to be self-aware. You have to assess your strengths and find where there is room for improvement. Honesty must come first and with it a desire to seek out those who will tell you what you need to hear—not what you want to hear.

An authentic leader does not have hidden agendas, they are genuine, vulnerable, and intentional. A Zen proverb illustrates this: The student says, "I am very discouraged. What should I do?" The teacher replies, "Encourage others." That is what leaders do, they listen to the concerns of their team members and offer ways for them to be more engaged and ultimately successful.

Patience is the hallmark of an authentic leader, while not paralyzing the process of making a decision. First, you let others know you have heard them and are committed to being fair-minded. Let your team members know that you want to hear various viewpoints and that you are committed to considering all options, and open to discussion before choosing a course of action. Those you serve will appreciate a consistent and dependable approach to decision making that balances sincere input while moving a group forward.

Authenticity means more than portraying your genuine self. A true leader has a set of values that others respect and want to emulate. Those values include being honest, just, even-tempered, and sincere. It is all too easy to ignore these traits in a competitive, fast-paced world in the pursuit of success. However, authentic leaders know any accomplishment is fleeting without the irrefutable desire to do the right thing.

## Servant Leadership

The other day, I saw a T-shirt that said, "You need to follow before you lead." I thought about that long and hard. The T-shirt represented an interesting way of looking at leadership. However, I want to turn that around a little bit as we think in terms of the servant leader. The leaders who are committed to serving those they lead are a critical element in authentic leadership. They are willing to leave their egos at the door and put themselves in a position where they are willing to ask questions such as:

"How can we help?"
"How can we serve?"
"What does the group need?"
"How best can we respond to those needs?"

After winning four FCS national championships, Chris Klieman was selected to take over for Kansas State University's Hall of Fame football coach, the legendary Bill Snyder. He was ready and began his first meeting with his players with the following phrase:

"You'll never hear me say, 'I,' it'll always be 'we.'" That's a servant leader—understanding the importance of the team—win or lose. I listen carefully to every press conference before and after each game. As he promised in that first team meeting, he always talks about "we," never "I."

The words we use count, and our actions are as critical as our words. The primary role of the servant leader is to provide a voice for those that have no voice. That's an important ingredient of authenticity. The servant leader puts his or herself in a position where they are carefully listening, and then providing an opportunity for others to be heard. That too is a critical part of being authentic. When we are committed to delivering on our promises, and exceeding expectations wherever we can, we are exemplifying the servant leader.

I gave my home phone number to hundreds of thousands of parents over the course of my career. Although ours is a large, complex university, I wanted to ensure that every single parent or guardian who had enrolled their son or daughter at our school understood that there was going to be someone there any time, day or night, 24/7, to help. This did not mean that I was going to solve the problem or concern right then, that most likely was a little more complicated, but our university made sure that there was someone there to be responsive and on the phone when they needed them most—that we were making a commitment that was authentic and sincere.

Author Tom Peters, in many of his books, talks about visible management: walking around and being accessible and approachable. That visibility is critically important. It is natural for us to want to see our leaders. And for us to truly see them, they need to be genuine as well as accessible and approachable. Insincerity is pervasive throughout our public and private establishments. It is becoming increasingly easy to see when someone is being disingenuous.

Servant leaders put themselves in a position where they're being responsive and adaptable as situations arise. They understand that they may need to put aside their own aspirations and lead by example. A servant leader is willing to put the needs of others first and set objectives that will be beneficial to followers and team members.

It is critical that we ask those whom we serve:
"What would you do if you were one of us?"
"What is it that you need?"
"How can we help all of us move forward?"

And then listen carefully to the answers. To be authentic, the servant leader must not only connect to the words, but to the genuine emotion of those we serve. The servant leader establishes an environment where the people he or she serves are open to express themselves honestly.

I had the honor to be the only administrator in our school's 157-year history to serve five university presidents. While each had a positive impact upon our school and me personally, one example of an authentic leader who created a supportive climate is General Richard Myers—a proud K-State graduate, four-star general who served as the chairman of the Joint Chiefs of Staff during 9/11. He is an American hero who, when he assumed the presidency at K-State, knew little about the nuances of leading a major, complex university system. Early in his tenure, on multiple occasions, when briefed about an issue (usually having to do with undergraduate students), he would think out loud on what should immediately happen to address the problem in a take-charge military fashion. Then, after taking some time to reflect, he would ask one of us in an unassuming tone, "Can we do that?"

He understands the importance of being vulnerable and seeking advice and counsel. He has the confidence to surround himself with staff who he trusts, and builds effective, winning teams that foster mutual respect. The members can express themselves openly, knowing they have each other's back.

Sincere authentic leaders know the importance of empathy, and one of the best ways to do that is through the sharing of personal stories. For example, during his daily briefings on the Corona virus, New York State's Governor Andrew Cuomo shared the pain of not being able to see his elderly mother and the fear he felt knowing his brother Chris had contracted Covid-19.

Another example is from the 2008 recession: While other companies were looking for ways to streamline, then Costco co-founder and CEO James Sinegal, approved a $1.50 raise for his hourly employees. He had empathy for his workers and insisted that, "…in a bad economy, we should be figuring out how to give workers more, not less."

Before writing my home phone number on a white board to thousands of parents of new freshman, I shared with them what the fall's new student class looked like. Many were the first in their family to attend college, so they had a lot of anxiety around choosing a major, finances, and finding their place in this new environment. Parents appreciate that their children's soon-to-be Vice President and Dean could identify with the students they were sending to this university.

I was able to relate to them because my first airplane trip was when I enrolled at Kansas State University. I was the first in my family to attend college. I was raised by a single mom and my dad had an eighth grade education. I began my college career as a mechanical engineering student, but graduated four years later with a degree in elementary education. I financed my education with part-time work during the school year, full-time work during the summer, and student loans. Sharing my own experience, let concerned parents know that the voice on the other end of the phone would be someone who "gets it."

Empathy is a key ingredient of a successful servant leader, someone who has infused this valuable commodity into the soul of their team, organization, or workplace. Building a unified, dedicated team starts with modeling the behavior expected of others and demonstrating the value of empathy in the work environment. It may not be a natural response for many, but training and supervision can convince even those who are the most strident, the value and satisfaction of being of service to others.

I am reminded of a political ad I saw back in the 1960s that illustrates true insincerity. It was for the governor's race in Kansas. One of the candidates was walking through a wheat field with his tie undone and his coat over his shoulder. He was looking up at the sky as the voice-over was talking about how this particular candidate resonated with both rural and urban citizens of Kansas. He not only lost the campaign—he got trounced. The commercial had all of the right words, but it was clear that the candidate did not have a connection with Kansas voters. No one in Kansas knew anyone who walked through a field with a coat and tie while looking up to the sky. His message lacked sincerity and authenticity.

As we think in terms of human relations, we earn grace or currency—human currency. That currency is valued, and it is all earned by the way we treat others, particularly when the people we serve need us the most and things are not going well. When there is disappointment or someone experiences failure, they must know they are in a committed, supportive environment. It is imperative that we are there when we win, but also when things are not going well. That is how we build grace and trust. That is when authenticity shows its true colors.

## The Characteristics of Authentic Leadership

Being authentic is more than just being nice or smiling at folks. Authentic leaders establish an environment where the people they serve in their organization or workplace feel empowered and understand the importance of responsiveness. That doesn't mean they are going to make everyone happy, it means they are committed to ensuring everyone is heard. Authentic leaders realize that while they cannot be all things to all people, they are still willing to be there and to help and support no matter the size of the organization.

Authentic leaders are self-aware and will develop their own styles and methods to stay connected with others. How can we make sure that we're sincere and very real for those who are looking for leadership? What does it mean to be an authentic leader in service to others? Below are some characteristics I have gleaned from leaders I have observed and followed:

Authentic leaders create welcoming and safe spaces.

Authentic leaders strive to ensure the composition of those teams and organizations they lead reflect those they serve.

Authentic leaders have a commitment to self-awareness and continue to educate themselves in the areas of diversity, inclusion, and equity. They recognize when faced with social or civic injustice that silence is as harmful as the acts themselves.

An authentic leader begins any conversation with the phrase: "How can I help?" and continues with "How can we help?" thus setting the tone of not "me" but "we."

An authentic leader puts themselves in a position of listening to those they serve.

An authentic leader is honest and doesn't claim to be the smartest person in the room. They have the confidence of knowing that they might not have the answer; that it may come from others.

An authentic leader attracts, retains, and encourages others. They possess the confidence to set the tone and know that sometimes they have to lower their own voices, which is a critical step to building trust in their team.

An authentic leader leaves room for compromise. They know that working on something together is what produces true ownership.

An authentic leader shares credit and gives credit to those who have brought a solution to a problem, or has helped the organization or group to move forward and recognizes individual efforts and contributions.

An authentic leader admits their mistakes, takes responsibility, and knows that none of us are perfect, and that we are all better than our mistakes. They are willing to acknowledge the disappointment they have caused and promise to make it right. It is not the mistakes we make, it is how we react to that mistake that defines us.

An authentic leader puts himself or herself in a position where they are always looking to be better.

An authentic leader sincerely wishes the best for others and means it.

An authentic leader promises little but delivers big, always striving to exceed expectation.

An authentic leader tells the truth.

An authentic leader embraces vulnerability and demonstrates right from the beginning that his or her purpose is to serve, not to be perfect.

An authentic leader looks outside themselves and within the group to pursue solutions that work for everyone and helps each member achieve personal and organizational goals.

An authentic leader is personally motivated to make a difference, has a sense of ownership, and is more interested in helping others more than themselves.

An authentic leader not only has the ability to grow and to be a better leader, but has the sincerity and willingness to be a follower when necessary.

Authentic leaders respond to emails and phone calls immediately, using the sender's or caller's name. The simple act of acknowledging them is important because it lets the individual know that they have been heard initially even if the resolution has to come later. I spent the last fifty years or so working with students, families, alumni and staff, conscious of being authentic and sincere while ensuring that my departments were doing the best job we could in serving others. There is nothing more embarrassing, in my opinion, than someone saying, "No one got back to me."

## The Art of Authentic Leadership

What does authentic leadership look like? What tools or ingredients does a person embrace that demonstrates they are committed to authenticity through creating a culture that develops others and has the motivation to serve others first in all that they do? Authentic leadership also requires the ability to see and articulate a problem.

One of the most important people in my life was Dr. Chester Peters. He was our university's Vice President for Student Affairs, and my mentor and advisor during not only my college years, but also as my first direct supervisor as a young professional. He spent time with groups of students, faculty, and staff, sharing leadership principles.

His advice was not theoretical. Whatever topic he was sharing with us came with specific examples to illustrate his point. For example, if he was talking about motivation, he would tell us about specific leaders and how they used motivation for their team members' personal growth. He shared with us different types of leadership styles and techniques. Regardless of the style or technique, all of the examples shared the importance of being authentic. The leadership skills could be applied to the workplace, families, institutions, and community groups. Developing these skills allows us to be more authentic and impactful in our daily lives.

He was a sculptor. His works started out as clay and when the shape was what he wanted, he carved them into wood. These pieces were more than art; he would use them to model various concepts to us. I was honored to be given one of those pieces that remains on my bookshelf. It is called "Creative Problem Solving," and is in the shape of an arch (like a table-size St. Louis Arch). Several carved pieces of wood make an arch and each piece is dependent on the piece below it.

As he designed the piece, he started with a block of wood with four sides. He explained that this first piece of wood represented the foundation for problem solving. Three sides have an eye carved in in them. Each eye is a different shape and made out of a different type of wood and represent different ways of looking at a situation and different points of view.

Through this representational lesson, Dr. Peters would show the importance of making sure that everyone has a chance to define the problem or situation from how they see the world. Seeing things from different sides is a fundamental part of decision making.

It is not only important for us to see things in different ways, but to listen to different points of view. How many times have any of us been in a situation, whether it's family or work, and before the situation is even examined, we immediately go to a solution? We haven't taken the time to listen and clearly define the problem, but we're already looking for a solution.

The fourth side of the foundational piece is blank—it has no eye. It represents those who do not see the problem or won't acknowledge that there is a problem. His final lesson: Leaders cannot assume everyone sees the problem.

If we are going to be authentic, it is important that we hear and see so that we don't go off and try to solve problems or respond to situations that have not been clearly defined. Most problems cannot be solved quickly. It requires listening and taking the time to ensure everyone impacted is given the opportunity to contribute their views.

## Transparency

One of the most important basic characteristics of an authentic leader is transparency. Today, more than ever, we're looking for leaders who are open, accessible, vulnerable, and understand the importance of sharing information to those that they serve.

Transparency does not just happen, it has to be intentional. One indication of transparency is the willingness to share information in a timely manner and in ways that can be understood. Rather than imposing our point of view, transparency allows those we serve to make up their own minds.

Sharing what we know in a direct and factual way can result in building trust, especially where there has been a lack of trust. Authentic leaders are willing to share that they don't necessarily have all the answers to the particular situation they have been called on to resolve. They are transparent so that as constituents, we can see they are making recommendations and decisions based upon the best information available to them at the time. They lay out the options and invite input. Authentic leaders do not shy away from showing vulnerability; they are willing to "leave their ego at the door," and admit they are not necessarily the smartest person in the room, but they know who has the information and the facts and are willing to turn to them.

Authentic leaders are willing to do whatever it takes to keep others informed and do not feel inconvenienced by that obligation. They will share credible information as it becomes available. As circumstances change, authentic leaders are forthcoming and able to explain the fluctuations in data and circumstances with credible information and details. By sharing data in a direct and meaningful way, authentic leaders are able to build trust among those they serve and depend on them. When people have clearly stated, accurate information, they are less likely to fill the void with assumptions or misinformation. Solving problems together allows for a sense of shared pride and ownership.

By leaving your ego at the door, inviting in the experts to share quantified data, and sharing information clearly, you are exhibiting true transparency. The benefits of transparency is that it not only allows you to solve the problem at hand, but improves the relationships you are building with others.

In the 1960s, I had the chance to see firsthand, New York State's Governor Nelson Rockefeller's town meetings. As a teenager, sitting in the back of a packed gymnasium of regular citizens, I observed how the governor responded to the questions raised by the citizenry. It was my first opportunity to observe a transparent leader. The governor would share the facts and explain the reasons for the decisions he made. His best trait was when he did not have an answer to a question posed he would say, "I do not know the answer, but we'll find out, and my staff will get back to you with the answer." I know first-hand that they did.

Vacations are an opportunity to get away from the stresses of life and my wife and I enjoy time in Las Vegas or taking a cruise. One of my favorite moments of a cruise is when the ship leaves port; it is a premiere example of leadership and cooperation as the crew goes into action as well choreographed as any Broadway musical.

One time, my wife Susan and I were on a cruise ship that was scheduled to leave port at 9:30 p.m. About ten minutes ahead of time, I was on deck watching, and waiting, for us to leave. At 9:30 nothing happened. At 9:45 we are still docked. At 10:00 we are in place. As we are sitting still, another ship next to ours leaves the port. At around 10:30, I noticed several people approach the dock, go up the gangplank, board the ship. A few minutes later, the gangplank is raised and the ship leaves port. There was no announcement of what happened.

I assumed there was some sort of mechanical difficulty, or a health-related issue, something very significant that prevented us from leaving. Since we were not given any information, all I could do was make assumptions. Turns out I was not alone.

The next morning, my wife and I were having breakfast when the *maître d'* approached our table. He told us we were invited to dine with the captain that evening. We had never been afforded that honor before and we happily accepted the invitation. That evening, we were seated at the captain's table and I found myself one chair away from an experienced sailor in charge of navigating a six thousand passenger cruise line.

The first question I asked the captain was: "What happened last night? We didn't leave port at the assigned time." He explained the reason as an innocent miscommunication that was easily corrected. I pointed out that there was no announcement, which left people to wonder and speculate about what was happening. He listened to my concerns about the lack of information and the rumors circulating around the ship, assuming the worse-case scenario. I continued by explaining that in my job in higher education, we do whatever we can to be transparent. We strive to communicate constantly through all available means to ensure that people who we serve, including thousands of students, parents, faculty, staff, alumni, and taxpayers are informed. We want them to understand what we're doing and why we're doing it. I shared with him why our university values authentic leaders who are transparent.

Well, four mornings later, at four in the morning, we were awakened by loud chiming and the captain's voice coming over the PA system. He said, "This is your captain speaking. We had a small fire on the seventh floor in a jacuzzi. It's completely out now and there are no other problems. I thought it was important to be transparent and to let you know that there was a problem and that it has been resolved. Have a good morning."

Susan turned to me and said, "He's talking to you! You made a difference in his leadership style and his way of communicating." I was appreciative that he took what I said to heart about being transparent and communicating in a timely manner.

When people don't know what's going on it produces negative energy. Most negative energy is unnecessary. It is counterproductive, creates an insecure environment, and is void of ownership. That is why it is so important, as we think about those we serve, we share with them in an authentic, sincere, and transparent way. In times of trouble or problems, it is okay to show our vulnerability even as we are taking ownership of the situation. When we show trust in the people we are serving, they in turn will give that trust and positive energy back to us. That is what transparency provides.

Transparency is a defining characteristic of authenticity. When information is shared in a timely and useful manner, it allows others to make up their own minds, establishes trust, reduces negative energy, builds ownership, and leads to making better decisions for those we serve.

**TEAMS**

## Effective Teams are Winning Teams

Hopefully, all of us have had an opportunity to be around great teams: groups of individuals who have come together motivated by a shared sense of purpose. The team reflects the characteristics of its leader. Regardless of how a team is configured, the team as a whole and each individual member should be committed to serving others in an authentic way. Teams that demonstrate responsiveness, inclusivity, and empathy have characteristics that should be celebrated, encouraged, and replicated. The team and its members are committed to the development and growth of others and are fully committed to a sense of purpose. We know how special that can be and wish it could be experienced by every group.

Members of a team are a reflection of their culture, which should be embedded in authenticity and the desire to be of service to others. This authenticity implies that each individual is committed to do their best at each and every opportunity presented to them.

From the time I was a paperboy at age eleven, to my retirement as vice-president and dean of a major university, I was fortunate enough to enjoy the full benefits of serving others and a commitment to encouraging others around me to be the best they could be. While not perfect or exhaustive, below are some of the important ingredients that help ensure teams and team members are as effective as they can be in a lifelong pursuit of being of service to others.

Effective teams understand why they exist, take ownership in the task ahead of them, share a singular purpose, and are committed to move forward together.

Effective teams work toward a shared mission or vision. They believe what they are working for is the right thing to do and for the betterment of others. They are confident that they have the skills to complete the mission.

Effective teams believe they are the best at what they do. They believe they are the best but not better. For example, as we established our recruiting program for K-State, we based it around the belief that our university is the best institution of higher learning in the United States. That does not mean that our school is for everybody. It does mean that students who choose to attend K-State will receive the best university experience in the country.

Effective teams have benchmarks to measure their successes and accomplishments. They are able to document progress and set higher goals. These benchmarks and goals reinforce their sense of purpose and give them renewed purpose.

Effective teams understand that they cannot be all things to all people. They embrace what they excel at and remain laser-focused on their defined service, program, or activity. Horseracing is an example of that kind of focus. The jockey and the horse are a team, their focus is on the finish line, doing the best at what they have been trained and practiced to accomplish.

Effective teams have a shared purpose and ownership. The individual members can't wait to attend a team meeting, and when they do get together, they don't want it to end. They authentically care about and respect one another. They understand why they are together as a team and what they are expected to accomplish.

Effective teams have a winning underdog mentality. Warren Bennis, in his book, *Organizing Genius: The Secrets of Creative Collaboration*, talks about the ingredients of winning groups. Those groups have an underdog mentality that's almost "them against us." They have something to overcome or conquer. This characteristic was often exemplified by the great teams that Coach Bill Snyder led at K-State.

As a team cited as the greatest turnaround in college football program history, Coach Snyder fostered a winning underdog mentality. The team had to face many adversaries in order to excel. Having a formidable adversary is a great motivator. Coke and Pepsi and Walmart and Target are business examples of taking on the adversary. Rivals make your team better because they give you something to overcome. Coach Snyder always understood the power of them versus us.

## Effective Followers

We often spend a great deal of time addressing the ingredients of an effective leader and defining leadership. Frankly, most of our interactions with groups are in the capacity of being a team member, a follower, not the leader. Therefore, it is just as important to be an effective follower—dedicated to everyone's success.

An effective follower must have a caring attitude. A shared commitment to the purpose of the group is vitally important. Dr. Jon Wefald, Kansas State University President for 23 years, often shared a lesson from a Minnesota minister. The minister divided the world into two specific groups: One consisted of people who cared for others, the other group only cared for themselves. President Wefald said he always placed his trust on the people who cared. The level of caring makes a great deal of difference in terms of effectiveness of any group. Make sure to surround yourself with individuals who genuinely care.

When facing a challenge, President Wefald would routinely place a higher priority on finding a solution… his emphasis was not on who or what created the situation, but, "What can we do to address what has or will occur?" While not totally ignoring the cause or finding blame, his approach to problem solving was a clear message of asking, "What needs to be done to address the situation, and who is going to step it up?" His management style created a strong, creative team that solved problems. We took great pride in anticipating negative situations, long before they became a concern, particularly when addressing obstacles that were in the way of meeting and exceeding expectations.

An effective follower is a team member who is always looking for ways to improve the group. There is a Navajo saying, "When you point a finger, three fingers point back at you." It means that it is impossible to point the finger of blame at someone without simultaneously pointing a finger back at oneself. Blame does not go one way, when you blame someone else for an outcome, as a member of the group, you are to blame as well.

An effective follower wants to bring something to the table—make a contribution. They are not depending on the leader to provide all the solutions to a situation or a problem. Being an effective follower means looking inward, searching for what they can offer to find a solution to a complex problem or situation.

An effective follower is willing to be vulnerable and is not afraid to say, "I don't know." However, they do not stop at the statement, "I don't know," but are willing to roll up their sleeves to find the answer to a question or a solution to a problem. They are committed to the overall purpose and wellbeing of the group.

An effective follower has a sense of urgency. They understand that timetables and processes will be formed so that expectations can be met. They are willing to be both physically and mentally present to ensure success.

An effective follower respects everyone else in the group and expects respect in return. They understand that there will be differences of opinion and are willing to listen and ensure that other voices are heard. They also provide voices for those that have no voice.

An effective follower has a sense of initiative. They are going to be the first to raise their hands to say, " I'd like to take on that challenge." They are willing to think beyond themselves and take a risk.

An effective follower is responsive to their environment. They are supportive of other team members' initiatives and successes. They have a winning mentality, but not at the expense of others.

An effective follower has a sense of caring, has initiative, respects others, is committed to others, listens to others, and has a willingness to roll up their sleeves to make the group better. These characteristics are also attributed to an authentic leader.

## Creating a Welcoming Environment

I've often heard a customer representative, or an employee on the other side of a table or desk or over the phone, complain about the "traffic," or object to the number of people that are coming through the door. Those comments might be a sign of an unhealthy environment. It would be helpful if everyone embraced the thought that customers are the reason they have their job or responsibility. Our obligation is to serve those who are coming through the door, or are calling or coming into our offices—those customers are paying our salaries.

I've been serving customers in one way or another for over six decades. I started, with the customers on my paper route and continued through the fifty years that I served students and their families at Kansas State University. They were all my customers and they paid my salary. As a paperboy, I treated every customer on my route as if they were my only customer, and, as an administrator, made sure every student counted.

It is an important distinction to understand that without customers, we don't have a job. We championed that philosophy throughout our Division of Student Life during my many decades of service. First and foremost, our job was to be there for the students as well as their families, and not only because they were "paying our salaries," but because it was the right thing to do. Our mission was not only to solve problems, but to anticipate problems. Anticipating problems was necessary to lessen the challenges our customers might face. Our job was to lessen their burdens and concerns so they would have a chance to be successful at our school. Being able to give others a positive experience has value far beyond economic. It is all about empathy.

A while ago, I met with the Kansas City Royals' player development group. They invited me to share specifically about how our university communicates directly with high school students. An important part of their marketing strategy is the draft, and convincing young people to possibly forgo or postpone going to college or community college in exchange for the experience of joining the Kansas City Royals baseball organization. They asked about specific strategies and techniques when it comes to working directly with young people.

The centerpiece of our successful undergraduate recruiting program at the university was the admissions representatives and their passion for serving others. This team of recent K-State graduates who had very successful undergraduate experiences both inside and outside the classroom, also had the willingness or desire to share their personal stories. They would begin interview sessions with prospective students by asking open-ended questions such as, "Tell me about yourself?" and "What do you know about K-State?" and "How can I be of assistance to you?" The interview was intended to shift from being a sometimes expected sales pitch about how great our university is to the needs and interests of the prospects and what ignited their interests in K-State. Admissions representatives were trained to answer questions that came not only from the students, but from parents and guardians by focusing on the student and keeping the spotlight on them.

Once they learned about the student's aspirations, goals, anxieties, and fears, they would first demonstrate that they had listened to the student and thought about what was being said before responding. Then, in a sincere and real way, the representative would share their own story, personal saga, and experiences. Having recent K-State graduates assume this role, they were able to share that not too long ago they were in the prospective student's shoes, wrestling with the same issues regarding how to select a college, pay for it, decide on a major, and other relevant issues. Having representatives who have had the same concerns and have felt the same vulnerabilities gives prospective students assurances that they are being heard, and what they have to say is relevant. This approach is part of our school's culture and the willingness to serve students and their families has been at our core for generations.

For the Kansas City Royals to replicate this approach meant engaging current and former players and their families to come and share their own stories honestly and in a language that was relatable to the prospects. In any recruiting effort, it is important to show empathy, that the feelings are shared and understood, and that answers are forthcoming.

We started a campaign a number of years ago where each fall we communicated throughout our university community that we welcomed new and returning students. Our slogan was: "We're glad you're here!" (with an exclamation point). We had flags, banners, and stickers and an overall feeling that we're welcoming students and families to our university community. And it wasn't just a slogan—we were, in fact, glad to see them and know them.

Back in the 1980s, we began answering our university phones with, "Welcome to K-State. How can I help you?" The person answering the phone would introduce themselves to the student or the family member by name. We wanted the person on the other end of the line to know we were there to be of service to them. Although the conversation was taking place over the telephone, we encouraged the receptionists to have a smile on their face, because that would translate to a smile in their voice. Even when not in direct communication, we were constantly thinking about how we could go above and beyond to serve our customers.

One day, I went into an electronics box store and was immediately greeted by an employee who asked, "How may I help you?" I am a technophobe, so I was pleased someone was right there who could assist me with my question. The employee took me directly to the product that I needed. I was out in two minutes time with my purchase. That made a big impression on me. I had been in another store, a person was at the front when I entered, but I did not know why, because they never said a word to me. They were doing their job, but I became a loyal customer of the store where the greeter went above and beyond to provide service.

Another time, I had a problem with a national shoe company and contacted them. I received a phone call back from Melissa from the Customer Relations Service Department of this major corporation. The fact that Melissa promptly called me back made a big difference. When I told her that I did not do well with technology, she said, "Well, you can go to our website and fill out your complaint and we'll make sure that we take care of it," I said, "Yeah, I'm going to have trouble filling that out." She said, "I'll tell you what, Dr. Bosco, I'm going to fill that out with you, we're going to do it together." Melissa listened. She understood and gave me a psychological "hug." It was great. In that moment, as she was sincerely listening to my frustration about their product and their recommended response to use the website, she made the decision to go the extra mile. She was personal, and she was intentional about helping me resolve a particular problem. That made a big difference. I'm going to go back and use that company again.

I have a favorite restaurant in Las Vegas that serves delicious clam chowder. I was eating there once and when the waitress brought me the soup, she also gave me a small bag of oyster crackers. I asked her if I could have some extra crackers, and she returned with a basket of crackers. She didn't just bring me an extra bag, but she brought me a basket, which exceeded my expectation. That was above and beyond service. Those little things count. We must appreciate the fact that customers can go anywhere and there's a lot of competition out there. The way we take care of our customers makes all the difference in the world.

At Kansas State University sporting events, when you drive onto the lot, the parking attendants always say, "Welcome to K-State! Enjoy the game." They are not promising we're going to win, but they are sincere about welcoming you there and wanting you to have a good time. They appreciate that you've come to support our athletic program. Their attitude makes a difference. Even before you get to your seat in the stadium, they have created that welcoming environment.

In terms of customer service, it is important to ensure that everyone who comes into contact with the customer has a sense of service and is committed to the customer having a positive experience in a welcoming environment. I remember a number of years ago, visiting with our university's indispensable custodial staff. I understood how critical their jobs were in ensuring our campus environment was clean, and just as important as the campus police who were entrusted with making our campus safe. Campus safety has become increasingly more important to families over the past few years and our university police understand the significance of establishing a safe environment. The food service workers, those who prepare food in the residence halls and other campus locations, are on the front lines of serving students, faculty, and staff several times a day. As they are serving up the food, they get a chance to look our students in their eyes. They know whether there might be a problem or not. They have to create an environment in that food line where students or others can share a concern or need. It is just another way they provide nourishment.

We established a "student of the year" award program to recognize student employees, and most importantly, their direct supervisors. These direct supervisors were mostly frontline staff members and were mentors to our students. They were often the first to notice a change in a student worker that might be effecting schoolwork or other aspects of their life. A student might go to them with a concern long before anyone else.

Regardless of the job or position, creating a welcoming environment and being of service to our customers is everyone's responsibility. That goes for internal as well as external customers. Everyone you encounter is either a customer or a potential customer, so acknowledging them, welcoming them, and offering assistance is imperative. It is an overall attitude of putting ourselves out there. A good example is Southwest Airlines. At the end of every flight an attendant says, "There are a lot of other airlines, you have a lot of choices, and we're happy and honored that you picked us.

Authentic leaders know their sphere of influence. We all know there are things we can't influence, but if you really think about it, you will discover a variety of areas where you do have influence that can be used in a positive way to ensure a welcoming environment to all your customers, whoever they may be, within and without your organization. How you interact with your customer must not be rote, but sincere and authentic. A welcoming environment is a caring environment, one that not only listens, but is responsive to the ever-changing needs of those whom we serve. How we are perceived by our customers makes all the difference in this competitive world, and they will be loyal to us if they believe we want what is best for them.

I read a book a while back called the *Fred Factor* by Marc Sanborn. *The Fred Factor* talks about a mailman and his extraordinary commitment to making sure that every single customer on his route is special and unique. It illustrates a commitment to going above and beyond the call of duty. To promise little but deliver big. We would train our campus tour guides, and all of our staff, when anyone asked for directions on campus, never to point, but to actually escort the prospective student or visitor or anyone asking for directions, to the physical location they were asking about. That was our way of making sure that we went above and beyond the call of duty. It's more than a smile. It's a commitment to solving a problem and being there when someone needs you.

## Delegating

One of the most important ingredients in our ability to create ownership and a sense of belonging is to be able to delegate responsibilities and tasks to others. The ability to take something seen as yours and give it to someone else to execute is one of the most important ingredients in the arsenal of leadership techniques. When you allow others to take responsibility and give them the authority to carry out specific tasks, you show respect and earn respect.

Delegating to others in your organization, be it managers or frontline staff, can be accomplished authentically and sincerely by following the steps shown below:

First step: Ensure the person you are delegating a task to has the resources necessary to be successful. The task must be attainable.

Second step: Have a timetable. Before you assign the task ask yourself if it can be completed within the assigned timeframe.

One of my first days working directly for Dr. Jon Wefald, President of Kansas State University, he called to give me a specific assignment. I was very new to the position and he and I had not had much time together, but I was happy to be entrusted with his assignment.

A couple hours later, I ran into him in the hallway and he said, "Pat, have you done what I asked you to do?"

I hadn't, because I put it on my "should do" list. I quickly learned an important lesson. When he assigned a task, it had to go on the "must do" list. His tasks had to be done with a sense of urgency. That was a mistake I made only once in the twenty-three years I served with him.

As a supervisor, you need to ensure that the person to whom you are delegating a task understands that it is obtainable in the timeframe you have defined. You won't be successful as a supervisor unless you have mastered those two important ingredients.

Third step: Clearly communicate with those around you.

There are individuals in your sphere who are familiar with your expectations and aspirations. They know exactly what you want and you may even be able to complete each other's sentences.

But not everyone in your organization or company is that familiar with you. You need to make sure that they clearly understand your expectations, which you should be able to put in writing.

Verbal and written communication skills are necessary to supervise.

Ken Blanchard's *One Minute Manager Meets the Monkey* is an excellent example of setting expectation. Any parent who has promised their child a puppy, has lived it. You bring home a cute cuddly puppy that your child adores, but you haven't explained what the expectations are of taking care of a dog. Before you know it, the dog still isn't house-trained, that feeding it and walking it takes a lot of care. The cute puppy is quickly growing into a bigger dog, within a few months, the adorable, cuddly puppy is a large dog that is hard to manage in your space.

Before assigning the responsibility of taking care of a dog you must know what is obtainable in your surroundings: How large will it get? When will it get fed? When will it be walked? When will it get its immunizations? How much time will be allotted to ensure the dog receives the proper care and attention? If the tasks are not attainable, then don't adopt the puppy.

Another example pertains to the last two minutes of a ball game when things appear to really happen. This seems particularly true of an NBA game. The truth is that coaches and teams prepare and practice for the end of the game. They have a specific, obtainable task to enact in a defined timetable and everyone is focused to make sure the plan is put into place.

One way to put this skill into your work is managing your manager. For example, if you're ever given an assignment, a wonderful approach to managing your manager is if you haven't received or been given a timetable, you should ask your manager or supervisor for one. Remember, success is a two-way street.

Fourth step: Reward performance.

There is a small voice inside of all of us that may understandably ask: "What's in it for me? What's the reward? What's the benefit?" No matter how altruistic we may be, it is important to establish a reward system. It doesn't necessarily have to be financial. You may not have control over pay or benefits or promotions, but you can still reward performance. It may be applause, a personal note of appreciation, sincere recognition at a staff meeting or gathering. Whatever it is, it is critically important to ensure that people receive credit for their work and what they bring to the table. A lot of business research concludes that there are more important, more motivational rewards to team members than money. In fact, money often comes up last on the list, while recognition of a person's impact—am I making a difference, knowing someone knows you are here—is consistently number one.

Fifth step: Honest evaluation.

A leader thinks in terms of the entire process and the path to success. Your responsibility does not end at the delegation of the task. Depending upon how the person is handling the assignment, it may become necessary to modify the assignment, assign others to it, or take the assignment away altogether.

If terminating the assignment is required, it must be done in a humane way. Things do not always go as planned and somewhere along the way, things may not have worked out well. So, when someone stumbles, it is important for you to be there to listen to what the person has to say and to provide productive criticism in an authentic, meaningful and sincere manner. Just because you delegated the task, it is still your assignment. As Harry Truman said, "The Buck Stops Here."

As you evaluate the situation and why the person given the task stumbled you have to ask yourself: "Why weren't they able to meet the expectations?" A self-reflection should include: "Were the expectations made clear?" "Is there an opportunity to correct the situation?" "Should the person be given another chance?"

Just as you are watching and evaluating the people who report to you, you are being observed by the people to whom you report. Just as you want to be encouraged to come forward and be honest when things are not working out, you need to offer that opportunity to your subordinates with sincerity and respect.

Management is an art as well as a social science. Managers are human beings, and as such we are not going to be perfect, the same is true for the people who report to us. It is necessary to have aspirations and set expectations, but we want to make sure that as we delegate responsibilities and ownership, we understand the assignment may have been ill-defined or poorly communicated.

Delegating a task or responsibility is a critical part of building trust and giving others a sense of purpose—that is how we build productive teams committed to specific shared goals and activities. In sports terms that is called: "Putting skin in the game."

The five steps shared here are a system that has worked for me. However, it is important that you develop your own way of delegating responsibility and authority, and create a process that works for you. What all authentic leaders share in common is that they are there for their teams not only at the beginning of the task, but also at the end.

## COMMUNICATION

THE KEY TO COMMUNICATION is the act of listening and creating an environment where anyone can ask questions, voice concerns, and make meaningful suggestions. Being willing to listen is an important part of building trust within a team. Keeping the doors of communication open is crucial.

Listening is the best way to build trust between leaders and team members, and that trust will allow for constructive criticism and reciprocal feedback. Constructive criticism is meant to be just that—constructive, and the feedback needs to be clear and detailed so that everyone else can learn from it. Feedback is a two-way agreement, not only is it given to others, it is accepted from others.

Effective communication does not make assumptions. No one can effectively complete an assignment if they are unsure what tasks they are responsible for. Everyone on the team must know the scope of the project and be clear about what is expected of them. Getting the team together regularly to check progress, ask questions, and address any issues is another good way to keep everyone communicating and assure that all team members are aware of their responsibilities to the project and each other.

Communication is not a "one size fits all" situation. Different situations require different ways of communication. For a project involving team members working remotely, a video conference may be an effective way for everyone to keep in contact about progress and milestones. For in-house projects, face-to-face meetings are often the best method of communication. Email has been a popular form of contact in the past few decades, but it can be inefficient and unreliable. Emails can get lost in cyberspace, sent to a junk folder, or overlooked in a crowded inbox and seem impersonal.

Not everyone communicates in the same way. For example, visual people tend to prefer written forms of communication while auditory people benefit more from a phone call, a video chat, or a face-to-face meeting. Recognizing which form of communication works best for each team member allows them to feel valued and willing to go above and beyond for the organization.

## The Power of Listening

Listening is the greatest psychological "hug" we can give another human being. Listening is the foundation for our interactions with others at home, in the workplace, in school, and in the community—anyplace you want to make a positive, lasting contribution.

This "hug" has no age requirement and produces positive results on everything from childrearing to establishing strong personal relationships, to building teams empowered to achieve greatness

We have two children. They're about five years apart, and the first born is "high verbal." When our second child was about ten months old, we decided that we were going to make sure that she would have high verbal skills so she would be able to communicate with the talkative Bosco household. We started by repeating back everything she said. If she said, "goo goo goo," we said "goo goo goo." If she said "gah gah gah," we all went "gah gah gah."

One Saturday afternoon, I was lying on the couch, reading the newspaper and listening to the Kansas City Royals game on the television. My daughter was sitting about four or five cushions away. She was chattering away, with her goos and gahs. Our responses to her had become rote so I was repeating the sounds. I was so absorbed in the paper and game that at first I didn't notice that she was moving towards me hand over hand. She got as close to me as she possibly could, took one of her little hands, put it on the pillow where my head rested, and pulled the newspaper away. Then she grabbed my chin, pulled it to her face and said, "Goo goo goo goo!"

What my ten-month-old toddler was trying to tell me was, "You're not listening to me!" It did not occur to me that a ten-month-old could tell that I was not paying attention. But anybody who we are around—including the people who we work for and work with, our family members, our siblings, our children, our neighbors and teammates—they all know when we're listening or not, no matter their age.

It is expected for those in leadership positions to be visible during crisis, when accessibility and approachability are needed the most. However, if they are only present during those times and have not established a routine connection with those they serve, it can be perceived as a token gesture that is insincere. Our staff would routinely circulate in the food centers; eat with students at the Student Union; walk the campus when classes ended, and walk with students to their next class; and make a commitment to speak to a student organization or living groups. We organized high school counselor lunches in every part of the state during the school year for decades. These counselor lunches always began with asking the front-line influencers, "What do you need from us to help you better serve your students?"—and then listen to their answers.

After we listened carefully, we would form responses that were direct, intentional, and non-defensive. Our authentic approach built trust and established long-term service relationships among these influencers. Being authentic also allowed us to feel the pulse of what high school students and their parents had on their minds. This was a different approach than other universities that were focused on telling high school counselors how great their school is and how fortunate a student would be to attend. We have learned that students and parents can sense insincerity a mile away. By taking the authentic approach, Kansas State University became the number one choice among Kansas high school graduates—a distinction we have held since 1986 (and still do today).

Listening and asking, "How can we help make a difference?" is illustrated in an example of a particular corporation the university was approaching for a major gift. At first, the corporation was not receptive to any of our proposals. After years of rejection, we were to the point where we were wondering if we should continue making presentations to them. Dr. Kirk Schulz was the President of K-State at that time. He was determined to get the corporation's support and I joined him in working on several proposals, some revamped and some brand new. We thought huge, and were prepared to present proposals that we thought would make a big difference to our university.

However, President Schulz, had a different approach in mind. At the beginning of the meeting he simply said, "How can we help?" He asked several executives from the corporation what their expectations were of us. He asked about their goals and aspirations, and how our university could achieve them. The executives were surprised, at first, they weren't prepared to hear this question asked, so they weren't prepared to share their aspirations and goals. They expected that we would lead as we always did, with our needs to advance the university. Instead we asked them their needs and we were prepared to listen.

When President Schulz addressed those executives he was authentic. He really wanted to know how our university could help them. That approach made the difference and it resulted in the school getting financial support for a variety of programs and activities. The big lesson was not to lead with your own needs, but to ask the important questions about the donor's needs and listen very carefully to the response to determine mutual needs and goals.

In the 1960s and 70s, college campuses were experiencing violent protests, canceled classes and programs such as ROTC and graduations. Students were killed (such as at Kent State) and buildings were burned (such as the University of Kansas Student Memorial Union). The mantra for young people was not to trust anyone over thirty years old. During that period, campus protests and student sit-ins at various universities were displayed every evening on the nightly news. Although Kansas State University had its own controversial and difficult times, the campus environment compared to other university communities had a different feel. There were students, faculty, and community members who were opposed to the war in Vietnam, the draft, and civil injustice, but their protests were always nonviolent and peaceful. What distinguished our university is that then President James McCain was always visible, accessible, and supportive of student engagement. He set a tone that was reflected throughout the university and community. While he may not have agreed, his message was always, "You are being heard."

His open door policy was legendary, and his staff was instructed to make his appointment calendar available to any student who wanted to meet with him. President McCain often delayed other important meetings so that a student or group of students could visit with him about their concerns and issues, which ranged from student aid to food in the resident halls, to how to invite the President of the United States to the campus to hear their concerns. During that time, it was widely documented that most college and university presidents distanced themselves from the student body. President McCain took a different path, he made himself available to listen. His open door policy sent a message that he was there to listen to the students and that he expected all vice-presidents and deans should do the same. He wanted to make sure that the students were heard at all levels at the university. He made it clear that Kansas State University was a student-centered university. Listening was of utmost importance and reinforced the university's commitment as a welcoming, caring campus.

The Sunday after the Kent State shootings, I received a call from the student body president at Kent

State University. He offered to come to our campus the following day and share with our students and university community what actually happened on May 4, 1970 that resulted in the death of four Kent State students. Classes were cancelled for the semester, and he was barnstorming to college campuses across the country. Unfortunately, he was only available the next day at 10:00 a.m. As Kansas State's student body president, I called President McCain at his home that Sunday evening and asked for his support. His first comment to me was, "What do you need?"

I explained to him that the Anderson lawn, which prior to my request had not been used for such a large, controversial event should be made available. We would also need a stage and a public address system in place by his 10:00 a.m. arrival. President McCain said he would make it happen. He also accepted my invitation to welcome those in attendance. I was pleased but not surprised by his acceptance, as he routinely addressed student gatherings with a message of encouragement, reinforcing our university's commitment to nonviolent protests and his famous open door policy.

That Monday morning, thousands gathered and heard a firsthand account of the tragic events that took place at Kent State University, all because our university's leadership demonstrated the power of listening to those they serve. On other campuses, buildings were occupied or burned, but not at our school. President McCain listened to the student body during a difficult period in our country. He displayed authentic leadership in a sincere and caring way by providing psychological hugs for students, faculty, and staff when they needed it most.

Accessibility, visibility, and a sincere commitment to listen to those you serve creates a supportive environment whether it is a family, a team, a workplace, or an organization. Even a complex major university with diverse backgrounds and points of view can be united to the greater good when they know there is a commitment to ensure that everyone, even those with no voice, can be heard.

It is important to have a fundamental commitment to be in the moment and focused so that we are listening to those who deserve our attention. They know if you are sincerely listening to them or not. The fact is, we let people know what we think of them by how we listen to them. Listening has to be intentional.

Think about leaders you have seen in your family, workplace, or government. Even leaders that we don't have physical contact with, can exemplify this skill, such as George W. Bush with the megaphone at the World Trade Center after 9/11 calling out, "I hear you," or Governor Andrew Cuomo in his Covid-19 updates providing psychological hugs by exemplifying his understanding of fears and concerns and responding to them with, "I get it," followed by facts and plans of action.

I thought about something Mindy Weixelman, Senior Director of our annual giving program taught me. She was the one who established the K-State Proud campaign with a group of student leaders years ago and organized the K-State Parent and Family Association. Her work illustrated the importance of building long-term relationships and the way to do that was through listening carefully to their expectation. She knew it was necessary to cultivate those relationships one-on-one.

Some of my most rewarding personal experiences were getting to know the donors who not only have been generous, but willing to make themselves available to give time and talent as well.

It is important to be aware of your expression and mannerisms when someone is talking. Is your attention on the speaker or is your mind someplace else? Are you giving the other person your undivided attention? Are they in the spotlight? Are you focused on what they are saying and how they are saying it? When someone is sharing an idea, question, concern, or information, your listening must be authentic and sincere.

Authentic leaders clearly demonstrate they are listening. I have a tendency to speak with my hands, but that can be distracting to others. One technique I use to demonstrate that I am listening is that I will sit on my hands to make sure that I am focused. That way I am sending the right message to those I am communicating with in a sincere, meaningful way.

The power of listening requires maintaining eye contact; being attentive, but relaxed; not formulating a response, but keeping an open mind; not interrupting to impose your solution; waiting for the speaker to pause and then clarifying what you heard; feeling empathy for what is being said; paying attention to nonverbal cues.

Listening is a learned skill and should be practiced until it becomes authentic.

## Communication

I spell communicate with Y-O-U right in the middle, so its: commYOUnicate. How we relate to one another is what makes *you* the most important word in the human language. Below are some helpful hints of how to be more authentic and more sincere as we cultivate our interests in working with others and serving those around us.

Listening is so important in the communication process. I saw first-hand how impactful a personal note can be to a recipient. I remember a handwritten note written in purple ink I wrote to an outstanding high school student who was disappointed she did not win one of our most prestigious scholarships. The competition was fierce, attracting the best and the brightest from around the country. Just getting an interview was a great accomplishment. I knew she would make a significant contribution to our school, and I wanted her to be a K-State Wildcat.

During her campus interview, she commented that she liked my purple car. For years I had my perfectly good cars painted K-State purple, and my vehicle was recognizable on and off campus. My note to this outstanding young lady included a "free ride" card in my purple car to be redeemed only if she became a Wildcat. She enrolled and was a standout, and became one of our most effective campus leaders. After graduation, this successful business woman traveled internationally, and continued to contribute to her community through her volunteer work and service to others.

Although we worked on several campus projects together, for whatever reason, the student never redeemed the ride in my purple car. Recently the mother of this alum sent me a note, reminding me of my offer nearly fifteen years ago. Her daughter was traveling overseas on business, but wanted to redeem the certificate when she returned home. It would be my pleasure and my honor to give her and her family a ride in my current purple car. A handwritten personal note can be far more important than you can imagine.

As we are intentionally listening to others with whom we communicate, it is important to listen to their emotions and feelings as well as their words. Communicating requires that as we attempt to influence others, that we never forget that we are interacting with a human being and that we are listening to the pulse and the emotional side of their challenges. When the other person realizes that we understand them and that we are being sincere, they will be sincere in their interactions with us.

The easy path is to want to come up with a message that will appeal to the masses, but people don't respond long term to general emails or announcements or newsletters or posters. Volunteers, committee members, employees, and students may get an overall sense of what you are trying to accomplish or inspire in them, but if you want specific feedback or action, then you have to be willing to speak to them one-on-one. To be an effective communicator, you must be able to speak with authority and sincerity, and always be willing to listen.

Studies have shown that a top fear for most people is speaking in front of a group. I remember being traumatized in my seventh grade social studies class. The well-intentioned teacher thought the student in the front row who aced all of his social studies tests would be a great person to read aloud the chapter of our textbook. So when she first called on me, I stumbled to the front of the room, embarrassed. I was not prepared for the task she had given me.

Effective communication requires being prepared. I prepare by writing out my speeches on a legal pad several times, and then focus on three or four points I'd like to make with an audience. I become familiar with the material until speaking about it feels natural. People think I'm speaking impromptu, but really, it's thorough preparation. Effective public speakers believe that before they get up in front of a group, that at that moment, they know more about the message they are about to deliver than anyone else in the entire world. Preparation gives you a sense of confidence and the authority to share the message you are about to deliver. That confidence also gives you passion and enthusiasm for the message.

It is also important to know how long you can hold the attention of those you are addressing. This will also help you with your preparation. For example, six minutes is the optimum amount of time to share three or four points with others. When addressing any group, it is important to make eye contact with the listeners and try to communicate with everyone in the audience. As well as eye contact, it is beneficial to make a physical connection. Instead of remaining behind a podium or lectern, move around the stage. Let the audience read your body language as they listen to your words. Keep an open stance and bring people from around the room into your presence. People want to feel included. Depending on the venue, use as much of the room as possible, sometimes I'll change the back of the room to the front of the room and walk around to make sure that I'm including physically as many individuals in the room as I possibly can. It's important when telling your personal saga or story, that there is a purpose to you being there. What is special about your message that others have not heard before. Show your vulnerability and how you've been personally affected or motivated by the message you're about ready to give. Empathy trumps almost anything.

Audiences want authenticity and sincerity; you don't have to be perfect, but you have to be real and sincere as you deliver your message. Audiences are looking for the "you." They need to hear and see themselves in your messages.

John Nesbitt in his book *Megatrends* in the 1980s predicted that with every high-tech innovation there would be a high-touch reaction. When we look at today's society and the instant responses through technology, we are still looking for that human interaction. That is why regardless of how the message is being shared, you are communicating to make a difference in others' lives and you are doing so in an intentional, sincere, and caring way.

## The First Question Should be "Why?"

Our first home was surrounded by beautifully manicured lawns. If you drove around the circle, you would see one beautiful manicured lawn after another—except for one—my house.

Our yard had very little landscaping, and the grass turned brown in the summer. I've never really given that much thought to my lawn. I don't care that much about it. But you know who cares? My neighbors.

One afternoon, I pulled into my driveway and saw a bag of fertilizer laying up against my garage door. I got out of my car, walked over to the garage, and saw there was a note attached to the fertilizer. It read: "Dear Pat, please put this fertilizer on your lawn to make your grass grow green and strong." It was signed by my neighbor Jim with a P.S. that said: "You owe me $15 and 23 cents for the fertilizer."

I got the "hint" and later on I went ahead and started putting the fertilizer on my lawn. I was working close to the curb when I looked up and saw a very little girl from the neighborhood peddling towards me on her tricycle. She stopped to watch me and then said, "Mr. Bosco, Mr. Bosco, why are you putting that stuff on your grass?"

I squatted down and started to explain why I was doing what I was doing. When I finished with what I thought was an awfully good explanation, she looked me in the eye with her big brown eyes and asked, "Why?"

I started explaining to her a second time why I was doing what I was doing. I stood up, walked over to the fertilizer bag and read some of the instructions out loud. I thought this explanation was even better than the first one. She remained seated on her tricycle, looked up at me, and again asked, "Why?"

I started to say something, but she just kept repeating "Why, why, why?" She wasn't being obstinate. I was reminded of the proverb: "When the student is ready, the teacher will appear." From this innocent question I learned something important about leadership.

It dawned on me that the most important question in terms of leadership is not who, what, where, or when, but *why* do we do what we do? The answer most often is: To have a sense of purpose.

It goes beyond asking, "Why?" We have to be willing to listen to the explanation. We also have to work alongside our co-leaders and our followers, and listen to them to ensure that we have a sense of purpose. That we understand: Why have we gathered together? Why are we part of a committee? Why do we go to work every day? Why is a teacher teaching that particular lesson? Why is the coach having the team do that particular drill? It goes beyond what our parents told us when we were kids, "Because I said so." That little girl made me realize I was treating the lawn because my neighbor said so, and maybe she was not ready to actually understand the reason why.

Effective coaches, teachers—all leaders—are able to tap into that feeling within all of us that motivates us. "Why" spurs motivation as we try to articulate the answer to the question "Why?"

Motivation is not about personal gain. It is about authenticity, sincerity, and a sense of care for those we lead. Whether I am a leader in one situation and a follower in another, I don't want to be a member of a group where I don't understand or connect to why I am there. Too often, we let fear or intimidation make us feel uncomfortable or awkward and that prevents us from asking the complete question: "Excuse me, can we revisit why we're doing what we're doing?" As leaders, we must anticipate that question of ourselves, we must know the answer to that question, and we should encourage others in our groups, classes, and teams to ask that question of us right from the start.

Once we are motivated, we will be ready to act. Before we act, we must define and develop a purpose and a process, one that generates buy-in from the group, class, or team. Buy-in is more than approval; it requires a willingness to be transparent about the process, and an allegiance to give and take in the defining of both purpose and process.

Once the "why" is defined, the motivation is expressed, and the process is identified, the leader must be able to instill commitment to see the process through to the end. This cannot be done from above or from a distance. It is imperative for leaders to roll up their sleeves and participate until the process is brought to its conclusion. Remember commitment does not come from the attitude of "Because I said so," but from the shared vision of "Because we want to."

## First Impressions

Making a positive first impression is a learned skill, more art than science. There's been ample research about whether that first impression takes five seconds, thirty seconds, a minute or two. While we may not know the exact number of seconds, we all know it is very short. More importantly, you only have one chance to make a positive first impression.

Whether we are introducing ourselves to an educational, employment, or volunteer opportunity, we must show an authentic desire to make a difference.

When you are given the opportunity to meet someone you should introduce yourself first, right out of the box. Prior to that introduction, you should know the social norms of the environment you are entering. Initially in Western culture, a firm handshake was the initial interaction. Now it could be a nod of the head, palms pressed together in the tradition of Namaste, or briefly place your hand over your heart. Even if shaking hands is no longer in favor, square your shoulders toward them, look them in the eye with a smile in your eyes, and listen intently.

Say your name and listen carefully when he or she speaks their name, making it the last thing you mention. For example, "It is nice to meet you, Mary; my name is Pat." Remembering the person's name is critically important. Focus on the person you are talking to and do not have another conversation or anticipated response in your head. Repeat the name of the person you just met and continue the conversation, using their name. Make sure you have the pronunciation right. If you are uncertain, ask them to repeat it. Show them that it matters to you that you say it correctly. If you are given a first and last name, do not assume you should address them by their first name. Use Mr. or Ms. or Dr. and let them invite you to call them by their first name or correct title. Don't assume you know the pronoun they want associated with them.

There are techniques you can practice if you have a tendency to forget names, such as association. For example, if the person's name is Jeff, and you like cooking, you could think Jeff rhymes with chef. If you're a fan of the movie star Jeff Bridges, you could picture him to remind you of the name. Maybe you went to school with a guy named Jeff who had a memorable physical feature like freckles. Picture Jeff's freckles to help you remember the name of the person you just met.

If you are going to be introduced to several people (such as an interview committee), you should have a plan for how you are going to stay in the moment and the technique you are going to use to remember several names. For example, drawing a circle and writing each name around the circle as they have shared it. Developing your listening skills should be a priority. Meeting someone for the first time means you are taking the spotlight off of you and moving it to them.

It is not enough to develop a technique, you must be authentic and genuinely interested in the other person. Look people in the eye when you are speaking to them and they are speaking to you. Remember the color of their eyes (which might help with developing a rapport). Take a moment to make sure that you are connecting with the people with whom you are conversing.

As well as making a personal connection, you should do the necessary homework to make an organizational connection. There are various online resources that will tell you about the organization's or company's brand, mission, and goals. These sites should also provide insight into the person or people you will be meeting, such as names, titles, tenure with the company or organization, where they attended school and awards or recognitions. Taking the time to gather facts demonstrates your professionalism and commitment, which gives you an edge.

Don't wait until you have an interview or initial introduction to practice first impression skills. Use your current associations, such as student organizations, fraternities, sororities, workplace, and even family gatherings to dress appropriately and practice eye-to-eye engagement.

## GIVING SERVICE TO OTHERS

THE PHRASE we have heard a lot recently is, "We Are in this Together." These words are more than a slogan. When we go into any venture with the intent of being of service and support to others, internally and externally, the task at hand becomes a labor of love rather than a laborious chore. That is the benefit of giving service to others—it comes full circle.

Giving is not about something tangible, it is about being open, engaged, and available. It is revealed in active listening, positive encouragement, modeling behavior, and intentionality. It is meeting and exceeding expectations. It is being aware of the well-being of others and offering assistance so they can meet their deliverables. That is done by:

Sharing knowledge

Understanding what is of value to others

Sharing resources

Sharing opportunities

Giving transparent feedback

Giving your time

The most important aspect about giving service to others is that it is done without expecting anything in return. It means putting the interest of others above your own in every environment: family, work, community, and organizations. Vulnerability is a trait of a stellar leader. Vulnerability doesn't make you weaker, it makes you stronger. It shows you are open and approachable, it puts others at ease, and as such, they want to be of service in return.

Harnessing negative energy in any environment towards service, and offering positive alternatives uplifts everyone.

## Respect

Authentic leaders are sincerely interested in others. They're approachable, they're accessible, and they have a sense of joy in helping others. They are constantly looking for ways to include others in a meaningful, intentional way. These characteristics are the basis of respect.

At Kansas State University I would teach the admissions representatives—often alumni volunteering their time—that their role was to represent the university. It didn't matter if they were meeting students in a classroom, library, cafeteria, or at a college fair. They were still expected to epitomize what it meant to be from K-State. That included respecting the moment—being the first to arrive at an event and the last to leave.

The volunteers (those who were able) were expected to stand in front of our displays at the assigned event and be friendly and personable ambassadors. It was important to us that they share K-State's legacy, including its status as the nation's first land-grant university with a reputation of being open, welcoming, friendly, and accessible.

My wife Susan and I had a chance to represent the university at a variety of official events. One of those events occurred years ago at the Kansas City Chiefs' home opener. The opening game at the Chiefs' stadium was a "big deal" in the surrounding area and the nation. What made the event particularly special is that the K-State marching band—The Pride of Wildcat Land—would be performing at halftime. Susan and I were selected by the university to represent our school.

When we arrived at Arrowhead Stadium, we were in our tried-and-true purple, although everyone else was adorned in Chiefs' red. We were escorted to the owner's box—a large, palatial suite on the fifty-yard line with food and beverages in a reception area. The box was two tiers and accommodated about two hundred spectators. We took our seats in the front row, excited about the game, but even more excited to see the K-State marching band.

Halftime came and the first thing I noticed was that everyone who had been sitting in their plush seats got up and went to the lounge area to partake of food and drink. Susan and I were the only two who remained in our seats to watch the halftime performance. The band had performed the day before at the annual Sunflower Showdown, K-State vs. KU where we won. We swelled with pride on that sunny day in Kansas City as our band prepared to take the field.

Just as they're entering the stadium, I looked out of the corner of my eye and saw a gentleman walking down the steps towards us. It was Lamar Hunt, the owner of the Kansas City Chiefs.

He came over and sat down right next to us. We watched the band and then he spent the rest of the halftime visiting with us. He told us how happy he was to have us there, how great our university was, and how important it was to have a K-State presence in the Kansas City area.

In other words, he took time to take the spotlight off of himself and put it on us, to make us feel welcome. Although the space was a sports stadium, he treated us as if we were in his home.

It was a great example of authentic leadership. Lamar Hunt, owner of the Kansas City Chiefs, demonstrated in a sincere, caring way, how important it is to be respectful of those that you meet for the first time. That is the same kind of respect that we ask our volunteers to show potential students.

When they represent us at alumni events, college fairs, or the State Fair each year. That is why we ask them to stand in front of our display, to be open, and inviting. We want our admissions representatives, who represent us in high schools around the state and around the country, to make sure everyone feels welcome, and we train them to make the temporary space their own so that they can feel comfortable in that role.

K-State is an open, friendly, responsive environment, and we want to make sure that we represent ourselves in that way—in a respectful way. Authentic leaders are our hosts and hostesses, no matter where they happen to be. You don't have to be Lamar Hunt, the owner of the Kansas City Chiefs, to show respect for those around you. You never know where your touch and your sincerity might make a difference in someone's life.

## Take the Initiative

There are times in life when we are given the opportunity to make our mark. It could be in the classroom, in the workplace, through community service, or within your family. Seeing opportunity and taking the initiative to fill the void is a key characteristic of a successful leader. Taking initiative means going above and beyond your role or job description, not only to distinguish yourself, but to make a difference.

A personal example comes from years ago, when I was an assistant dean at Kansas State University in the early 1970s. Back then, I was pretty "low" in the university's hierarchy. At that time, the university was not promoting itself in a unified manner. One spring, the school was hosting an open house, which was specifically for the College of Engineering. Although it was a great activity, it skewed the perception of what the entire university was all about.

The university had another open house in the fall, during football season, which was for the College of Veterinary Medicine. These open house events were held department by department, rather than showing the university as a unified institution.

I decided to take the initiative and suggest to the Kansas State University President at the time, Duane Acker, that K-State organize an event for the entire university family. It would include all of our colleges, living groups, student organizations, students, faculty, alumni, parents, and families. They would all come together on a designated Saturday in the spring to showcase the breadth and scope of our comprehensive and diversified university, including academics and student life. The intent was to give prospective students and their families a comprehensive view of this great land-grant university.

It is easy to come up with ideas, but to turn ideas into action requires initiative. I do not know if the president thought I would be successful, but he appreciated my initiative. I had the desire, commitment, and skills to make this event happen. As an assistant dean, I had access to the entire university. I was given the opportunity to bring anyone associated with K-State together in what became the Kansas State University All University Open House. This annual event now attracts over 20,000 on the given Saturday. It also became a model program for other colleges and universities.

The event was a benefit for the university, and it allowed me as a young professional to distinguish myself to the senior administration. I suggest, regardless of where you are in an organization, you look for those opportunities to demonstrate initiative. Know what is going to be required to make it happen and be committed to go above and beyond your job description. Taking initiative goes beyond your day-in, day-out job responsibilities. It is more than just doing a good job; it requires putting yourself out there and taking a risk. You have to believe in yourself that you can do the unexpected. Your motivation is not just self-aggrandizement, but something that will move your organization forward.

Looking over my career, many of my direct reports were interim positions where the incumbent probably years earlier had caught my attention by demonstrating initiative. I saw them take a risk, or be the first to raise a hand for an assignment outside of their job description and then deliver. Those are the people who inspired me.

People in supervisory positions are looking for individuals to solve problems, who want to prove themselves by doing great things or things that no one else wants to do. These are unique opportunities that give you a chance to distinguish yourself in your career or community organization in a strategic and intentional manner. These opportunities expand your outlook, give you confidence, and offer the opportunity to work "outside of the box." Taking initiative is a source of great satisfaction as it lets you and others know that you are bringing value to the organization.

## Paying the Debt

Sometimes we're just in the moment and that's important. However, authentic leadership calls for something more: It calls for us to plan for the next generation.

We should ask ourselves what it is going to be like after we leave, after we move on. "What have I left to build upon?" Asking this will allow each of us to be more authentic and more impactful in our daily lives, whether we're working within an organization, interacting with family members, or finding ways to respond to the day-to-day challenges of everyday life.

Think for a moment how your entire orientation changes if you're thinking about not only the present, but the future. Looking forward helps an organization you care about have sustainability. You learned how to problem solve and address challenges in a competitive and challenging world in ways that can be passed on to others.

Having an orientation of, "What can I do, not only today, but what does this do for our future?" changes the way we look at the world. It gives us a chance to not only be in the present, but to foreshadow and care about decisions we make today and the implications for tomorrow.

Part of my fraternity's ritual is a phrase called "Paying the debt," and I'm sure it's not unique to a fraternity or sorority or to an organization that cares about the next generation. But the ritual calls for a commitment to always be looking for someone that's going to join our organization—someone who is going to be a little bit better than you, someone who can take us to the next level. Constantly looking for someone who will contribute more than you—is being forward thinking.

The beauty of looking for your replacement is another way of saying that your role is not complete until you find your teammate, much like handing off the baton in a relay race, hoping the next person will be even faster. Until you find your replacement, your role isn't quite fulfilled, because you have an obligation to ensure that there's a foundation and there's a next generation.

Mabel Strong was a residence hall director for a number of years at K-State. She made such a meaningful contribution to the university that the Strong Complex on campus is named after her. Mabel had a campaign each year called "Kiss a Frog." It was her take on the fairytale where by kissing a frog you may turn it back into a prince or princess. This change symbolized for her that one person's actions could make a difference.

She would challenge current school leaders to look around for someone to touch, to "kiss," so to speak, and encourage them to get involved. It was her way of ensuring that there would continue to be leadership where students intentionally looked for the next generation of not only leaders, but effective followers and team members to serve throughout the university, and that they were constantly paying it forward—"paying the debt."

## Thanking Your Heroes

During my senior year at K-State in 1971, I was a student teacher at Marlatt Elementary School in Manhattan, Kansas. I was assigned to Mr. Don Brown's sixth grade class. I learned a lot from Mr. Brown, a wonderful teacher, but I even learned more from his former students.

The relationship to Mr. Brown, this great man, made a significant impact on me and how I see the world. Like most teachers, he and I would spend several hours at the end of every day preparing for the next day. On most of those afternoons, something special and life-changing would happen: Former students, from middle school, high school, some in college, even a few adults would stop by unannounced. Their only agenda was to be back in Mr. Brown's classroom where they could give and receive a hug, ask a question or two, or to catch up with a person who made a difference to them.

Some would say "thank you" for being a positive influence, acknowledging the impact he'd made in their lives. For others, simply returning to a place and to someone who made them better was just the comfort they needed.

On occasion, after an impromptu visit, I asked Mr. Brown what those visits meant to him to have former students dropping by with nothing on their minds other than to pay their respects. "These visits meant the world to me," he said, "they're defining moments."

Those former students were thanking a hero—an educator. Seeing them come into Mr. Brown's classroom validated my career choice where I would be given the opportunity to make an impact on the lives of others. I hoped that someday my students would let me know if I had done a good job for them. I was humbled when former students acknowledged my impact on them.

It doesn't take much to thank our heroes, but it is a definite call to action. It could be taking a few minutes to make a phone call, schedule a visit, write a personal handwritten note, send a card or a text to someone who made an impact in your life. Those few minutes matter.

Several years ago, after my student teaching experience was long over, I visited Mr. Brown's classroom. He was sitting at his desk preparing for next day's class. Not surprisingly, he was in the company of two former students. They were there for the very same reason I had come: to say thank you to a hero. I had to wait my turn, but it was worth it.

I recently attended Mr. Brown's memorial service. I spoke to his family about the impact this great man had on me. Surprisingly, they already knew that impact. You see, Mr. Brown, at some time during his life, shared my remarks, my feelings, with his family. It had that kind of an impact on him. Knowing that meant more to me than anything, and made me wonder *Gee, what would've happened if I didn't take a moment to stop by his classroom and let him know what he had done for me?* I would have regretted it.

There is no room for regret if you thank your heroes. Do it now with sincerity and authenticity.

## SETTING GOALS

IT IS GOOD to get a sense of what individual members hope to accomplish. Team members are motivated when they feel they are heard and are involved in something that relates to their personal goals. That does not mean they get to do only what they want to do, but that they are personally invested in the team and willing to work toward shared milestones and achievements. All goals must be specific, measurable, attainable, relevant, and time-bound.

Below is a process for goal setting:

Identify the goals through brainstorming

Reach consensus and write down the goals

List the benefits and obstacles of each goal

Create and share an interactive action plan

Implement actions

Review progress on a timetable

Make adjustments based on shared information

Accountability keeps everyone on track and may take the form of checklists and reports. Each team members' tasks and micro tasks are known by all of the other team members and progress is shared openly. Sharing progress lets everyone see how individual efforts contribute to the overall goals and the path to achieving them collectively.

Goals must be quantifiable and not vague. Each goal should have specific measurements that monitor the progress toward the goals and when certain milestones should be met. This is often referred to as an action plan. Team members should contribute to the action plan, which furthers accountability.

## Goal Setting

Setting goals, dreams, and aspirations with timetables and deadlines makes all the difference in the world as we attempt to move organizations forward. As a university administrator, I've been around some very complex goal-setting strategies and techniques. Some of them have gone well, but some have not. There are some common denominators as we think about effective goal-setting. There are some straight forward things that can be done regardless of how sophisticated a system happens to be. It is important that we make sure that we are authentic, sincere, and intentional in our goal-setting. There needs to be an overall vision that authentic leaders set—a vision that defines success in both specific and broad terms.

Our Hall of Fame coach, the legendary Coach Bill Snyder, had a clear vision for his football team to "get better every day." We can all improve a little bit every day. He contended that the vision had to be operationalized, and that process needed to be bottom-up. He wanted his players and anyone associated with the program to get better each day. He empowered each of them because they were the ones who would be implementing the day-to-day challenges as the team and the university moved forward.

A vision must be more than an idea. It must be operationalized so that the individuals who are directly affected are involved in the goal-setting process. As simple as that sounds, oftentimes, that doesn't happen. We had a university administrator several years ago that simply sent out a memo that said: Set goals for everyone across the university. The administrator's vision did not last very long, but there was a life lesson in the failure. I observed Dr. Jon Wefald during his tenure as president of Kansas State University on many occasions. He established an overall vision and communicated it in ways others would embrace. He allocated resources with authority and responsibility that allowed those around him to be successful. His was an authentic formula that could be modeled by anyone who desired to move an organization forward.

For a vision to take hold, it is necessary to make sure that genuine ownership is identified and that goals are set. The vision is best defined simply by the individuals who are actually working day-to-day to make things better in their organization. But does this happen? I would ask staff about their goals and aspirations. Our vision setting began with a blank sheet of paper. For example, if the vision was about putting students first, then the staff needed to support that vision by presenting their goals with measurable deadlines. Checkpoints were also put into place. For example, admissions representatives could evaluate their progress by setting the vision of maintaining that the university remain the number one choice of Kansas high school students. They wanted to see where they were halfway through the year and if they were making progress or needed to make adjustments. They wanted to take stock to ensure they had goals that were reachable.

It is also important to be transparent about visions and goals. Part of goal-setting is to share those goals with stakeholders—those who are going to be most affected and motivated once those goals have been established. The stakeholders need to see that the goals are measurable and attainable, and the right amount of effort is in place. Part of our job as project managers is to make sure that we are in fact owning the process and ensuring that we're helping others be successful. Vision and goal-setting can be applied beyond organization.

For three decades, I coached a competition traveling fast-pitch softball team. They would meet at second base before each game. They would huddle around the base, arm-in-arm, and express, one at a time, what they would like to do to help the team be successful and what their personal goal was for this particular game. The players called this pregame exercise the "Field of Dreams."

Every New Year's day, my family would set family goals. My wife and I would sit down with our children and we'd talk through how we could make our family better this next year. As we worked through our goals, we made sure they were measurable in some way, and then we'd go ahead and list them on the refrigerator door so that anyone coming into our house could see the Bosco family goals for the year. Oftentimes, our goals had a lot to do with communication and improving quality of life as a family. What was most important was that we worked together as a family to improve our togetherness—our connection.

At Kansas State University, the 2025 university strategic plan was a bottom-up strategic plan. We realized for us to get better as a university we needed measurable goals that we were willing to share with others through a website. Our vision had a very sophisticated bottom line, which was that we involved everyone: from the lowest level to the highest level of the university. Our plan included periodic feedback. We had benchmarks that gave us a chance to revisit our goals and modify them as needed. For example, our Division of Student Life fundraising goal was to raise forty million dollars for student success programs and student scholarships. We established that goal by going department by department and asking what we could raise, what was reasonable. When we reached that forty million dollar goal, we rewarded ourselves with a party and congratulations. Then, we went ahead, and after a lot of input, made another goal, increasing our goal from forty million to sixty million dollars so we could include a Welcome Center. We continued to provide opportunities for periodic feedback to see how things were going—what was working and what wasn't working. When we needed to, we huddled up for team meetings to give ourselves a chance to see how things were progressing and to help support and get support from management, groups, and individuals. These hurdles gave us a chance to check and see if we wanted to modify any goals and strategies. It reinforced that we are in this together.

An important part of setting goals is to make sure that as well as evaluate, we reward ourselves and our team periodically. It's important to look back at achievements and celebrate them. It's important to acknowledge not only our challenges but our accomplishments. We need to share openly and honestly and allow ourselves to regroup if we have to and do better the next time. That's part of the cycle of life in an organization. We have an opportunity to come together as a group or as a family and recognize what we've accomplished.

In *Alice in Wonderland* there's a wonderful scene where Alice is up in a tree just talking to the Cheshire Cat. She has to make some decisions: she can go this way or that way. The Cheshire Cat looks up and says, "Alice if you don't know where you're going, any road will get you there." Without specific goals, as we've seen it in every aspect of life and every organization big or small, if we don't have a sense of where we're going, any road will get us there, but where is there? Goal-setting is an important strategy in helping us define our success and getting us where we want to be.

## Attention to Detail

Authentic leaders have a commitment to detail—an opportunity to dot the i's, cross the t's, and establish a creative, supportive environment where details are critically important.

I always appreciate it when I encounter someone who reinforces these life notions.

Several years ago, I was checking into a Kansas City area hotel at about 4:30 in the morning. As usual, I was wearing K-State gear. While I stood in line to check-in, a gentleman in front of me was checking out. He turned around and saw me in my K-State gear and asked, "Do you happen to know coach Snyder?"

He was referring to coach Bill Snyder, the legendary K-State football coach and Hall of Fame recipient. I said, "Yes I know the coach."

He said, "I played for coach Snyder at the University of Iowa. I was a wide receiver."

"That must have been a tremendous experience," I replied.

"It actually was," he said. "Let me tell you a quick story: I was a sophomore and we were getting ready to play The Ohio State University. During practice, I went out for a pass and I caught the pass with my arms extended out. Coach Snyder was their offensive coordinator at the time, and he stopped the practice. He said, 'You caught the ball in the wrong position. You should have caught the ball closer to your body.'

"This surprised me because I was proud of the catch I had made. He explained to me that while I had caught the pass, I did not do it correctly. 'When you started the play, you were a half-inch off the line from where we told you to stand, and that resulted in you not being able to make the catch where we wanted you to make the catch.' I responded, "But Coach, I made the catch.

"He went on to explain, 'That's not the point. I want you to catch it appropriately, in the right spot. It means starting a half-inch closer to the line than what you did.' He had me run that play three times and each time I caught the ball closer to my body. I was able to do that because I started exactly where Coach Snyder asked me to: on the line, a half-inch closer.

"An hour later, the entire team was in film study with Coach Snyder. He stopped the film session to show everyone how I had inappropriately started the play a half inch off the line, which resulted in me catching the ball, but not in the appropriate manner, and that it needed to be closer to my body. To emphasize that detail, he ran that film three times in front of the whole team."

I asked him how that made him feel.

"Attention to detail is absolutely important in terms of our ability to be successful. I became an All-American at the University of Iowa because of the attention to detail the coach had provided. Now, I own my own company. I use that same philosophy of attention to detail the coach shared with me during my sophomore year when I thought catching the ball was all that needed to happen. He taught me that attention to detail makes all the difference in the world. I know, because not only have I been successful, but that principle has been imparted on those who work around me and has helped them to be successful as well."

Think about how this philosophy has or could impact you in work, with your family, or with your community activities. Have you ever felt offended when someone made a comment about a decision you made? Often times it's not the decision, but the process about how you came to that decision.

Process is critically important and requires paying attention to detail as part of the process. If you come to a decision without working through the process, you may make a "lucky catch," but the outcome will not be sustainable. It's not just the decision, but how the decision is made that makes all the difference in the world.

## What Ifs

Posing the question "What if?" as part of your goal-setting strategy enables leaders and their teams to change or modify assumptions and make more informed decisions as their plans unfold. What if can be used to try-out scenarios and optimize a plan, because it provides the team with possible consequences. They can range from a simple evaluation of the impacts of changing one or more of your team's planned activities, or be used as a more complex exercise.

What if is a question asked to explore possible outcomes. The following list is an example of "What Ifs:"

What if lead time for a deliverable is extended?

What if another team we are depending on doesn't follow through?

What if we need to extend the duration of certain activities to ensure quality?

What is the effect on those depending on our services if unforeseen circumstances arise?

What if we reprioritize our tasks?

What if we accelerate the schedule?

Answering these questions quickly, reviewing the results, and asking new questions is the process by which leaders and teams find the best solutions. The questions often involve making changes to data, running analysis, examining the predictions, comparing it to the schedule, and then challenging the effect.

A few months ago, I was asked to attend a meeting with the leaders of public education for the State of Missouri and the State of Kansas. The meeting was all about how can we create an environment within public schools, in both states, that gives students a chance to be better at creative problem solving, to deal with the "What Ifs."

I was honored to be at this historic joint meeting to address what we were all interested in doing, namely preparing young people for today's complex world. Creative problem solving certainly is one of those important characteristics.

I remember a trip to Buffalo, New York with my dad. I was about eight years old and in the afternoon, he took me to the zoo. This was in the 1950s and the zoo exhibits back then were nothing like what my grandchildren enjoy today, and even for the 1950s the zoo was old and antiquated.

I remember entering the reptile building. The smell and the noise was just incredibly repugnant, but I wanted to be in the reptile building with my dad. All of the exhibits were behind glass in aquarium cages along an aisle. It was protected by rails that were installed to keep visitors away from the glass exhibits.

The first three or four exhibits had large reptiles in them, and kids were hanging on the rails and banging on the glass. They were yelling at the snakes and the alligators and the lizards that were on the other side of the glass. However, in the middle of the building, nobody was pounding on the glass and as we got further down the aisle, we noticed why.

On one of the exhibits a note was taped to the glass. I was eight, and beginning to read and my dad helped me read the statement: "Don't bang on the glass. What would you do if the glass broke?" That stayed with me for a very long time, the "What Ifs." What would have happened if the glass actually broke and that big, giant, brown and green snake got out? For an eight year old, it was memorable.

I started thinking about this whole business of how we establish a creative, supportive environment where the people that we serve understand that we need to examine the "What Ifs." What happens if we go this direction or that direction? What are the implications?

I remember studying a Japanese style of management a number of years ago that addressed not only short-term, but long-term implications of a decision that we make today, the "What Ifs." How do we anticipate impacts and outcomes?

Authentic leaders do what they can to create a supportive environment. One that gives everyone a chance to explore in a positive way what happens if we go this direction or that direction, and to anticipate the positives and the negatives of any decision that we make.

As we discussed at our joint meeting of educators, classroom teachers employ team building exercises and case studies that complement subject matter, and at the same time, expand a student's ability to solve problems creatively. We also recognized the impact work, internships, and extracurricular leadership activities play in the development of a student's capabilities to ask the "What If?" questions. They are encouraged to address solutions to complex questions innovatively. Activities such as sports, music, student clubs, and publications, academic competition teams, community organizations such as 4-H, and student government can provide real life leadership experiences. These experiences challenge personal beliefs and values, move a student outside of their comfort zone, and allow mistakes to be made, which are not life-threatening, but gives the student a chance to develop and refine their capacity to ask questions and provide answers to the issues of the day.

Years ago, we started the All University Open House program, where over 2,500 volunteers, students, faculty, and staff organized an extraordinary weekend of exhibits, programs, and activities to showcase what K-State has to offer in the classroom, in our labs, and also outside the classroom. These offerings included our student organizations, our campus activities, living groups, and the like. Activities were planned for inside and outside. It rained the entire time and all the outside exhibits were gone.

We didn't explore the "What Ifs." We did not have a contingency plan for if it rained the day of our All University Open House. We assumed that God would not let it rain on a purple day like that, but he or she did. We learned from that experience and established a contingency plan of "What Ifs."

Championing student leadership and involvement through advising, coaching, and training has been a significant part of my professional life. I encourage students to roll up their sleeves and to make their environment better than when they first arrived—that was very important to me. However, my underlining motive was always to use outside classroom leadership experiences as a vehicle to improve students' ability to become better problem solvers. For any student-led group that I advised, it was not about encouraging the student leader to be the best all-time president or leader of a group; my sole purpose and belief was to provide real-life opportunities for making a difference. My intent was to engage them and help them to become the best educator, entrepreneur, healthcare provider, life partner, U.S. Senator, engineer, parent, partner, and/or citizen they could possibly be in life.

Learning to ask the "What Ifs" is just as significant as learning to anticipate challenges and concerns long before they become insurmountable for those the leader serves. Education is the cornerstone of this skill as it is educators who understand the power of engagement in and outside of the classroom. Educators in any setting understand that engagement is key to a student's ability to creatively address problem solving.

As "What Ifs" are explored, authentic leaders are open to suggestions not for whining or complaining. "What Ifs" are about options and not about looking for the negative, but positive alternatives. This gives team members the opportunity to add value to a complex challenge.

Authentic team members understand the dynamics of complexity and want to offer positive contributions as we explore and anticipate what could happen. What the "What Ifs" happen to be in any kind of a challenge or opportunity makes a difference to the overall outcome.

Asking "What If" questions provide an opportunity to develop predetermined, possibilities in order to test how projected plans will perform under varying factors and controls. "What If" scenario planning allows a team to respond to alternative situations more quickly and effectively, because they have developed strategies to minimize the impact of changes and thus reduce uncertainty about the future.

A "What If" scenario is an informal speculation about how a given situation might be handled. The more questions that are asked, answered, and reviewed throughout each stage of the project lifecycle, the more informed the leader and the team are to offer more predictable outcomes.

Another benefit of utilizing a "What If" scenario, is that it is a straightforward method to address basic questions and extract necessary information more quickly.

Goal setting and project planning will always be impacted by a degree of uncertainty, especially in an environment subject to internal and external circumstances. The challenge is to manage these circumstances and uncertainty through thoughtful consideration of how these situations can have the least impact on the group or organization.

"What If" analysis allows teams and leaders to recognize options and impacts from various events and ever-changing situations by observing and reasoning, so better predictions of outcomes can be made.

## Be Open to Change

It is easy to become set in our ways, but rigidity against change can be detrimental to progress. Change does not mean losing our sense of self or abandoning our values, it is an opportunity to be flexible so we can adapt circumstances that impact our lives.

In 1989, Coach Bill Snyder became the football coach at Kansas State University. As the new coach it was understandable that he had a list of things he wanted to make sure were put in place at K-State. One of those was a logo for the football team—something special and unique. I was invited to his office in the spring of 1989, where he asked me to look at drawings of what eventually would become our Powercat. As I looked over the four or five sketches all I could think was, *This new logo will be something special for the football team.*

As long as I could remember, the K-State's logo was Willie the Wildcat or "Stand Up Willie" with the flag. That was my Willie—the university's logo when

I was an undergraduate here. As an administrator, I often used Willie the Wildcat for recruiting and public relations programs. I supported that Coach Snyder might want something different for the football team, and early on I took it as such.

Four years later, just after our first bowl game, I went to the Student Senate with an ID card proposal. It was the first time in school history we were going to have a plastic student ID card. It was intended to replace the paper card that demonstrated a student had paid their fees. We had partnered with a local bank to provide us a card with a magnetic strip. We had the technology in place to utilize it and the university and Student Senate were excited about the "high-tech" card.

During an early planning meeting with members from our Student Senate, one of the students asked what would be on the ID card besides the student's signature. I said, "Well isn't Willie the Wildcat our symbol of the university?"

A silence fell across the room and I could tell by their body language that some type of disagreement was brewing, so I asked, "What's going on?"

The response I got was, "Well, the Powercat ought to be on our ID card."

"Isn't that the football logo?" I offered. "Willie the Wildcat is our university logo." The argument went back and forth until I finally said, "Well, I'll tell you what, there's an SGA election coming up in March. Let's put it on the ballot." The Student Senate agreed, and we put the logo choice of Willie the Wildcat or the Powercat before the student body to decide which one would be on the Kansas State University student ID card.

Willie lost five to one. Ever since, the Powercat has proven to be the most recognizable symbol of our university. I learned I had not been the most flexible person in the room. I had been resistant to change. I also learned that it is important to recognize that you need to listen and respond accordingly to any situation.

I had convinced myself that Willie the Wildcat was the recognized logo of K-State—the symbol of our school, because that's how I saw it for years. The twist was that in just one year, and every year after, over a million dollars is raised from the licensing of the Powercat. Those licensing funds are used for scholarships, to support the marching band and other student initiatives.

I will always be grateful to Coach Snyder for introducing the Powercat to our university, which has become one of the most recognized logos in the nation, and for showing me the importance of leaving your ego at the door.

## SUCCESS

*"Success is peace of mind, which is a direct result of self-satisfaction in knowing you made the effort to do your best to become the best that you are capable of becoming."*
—Coach John Wooden

SUCCESS IS NOT DEFINED by the amount of money in your bank account or how many things you have acquired. Success is an attitude of well-being that you are able to share with others. As you and your team take on a project, or are tasked with other ways to represent your group or organization, it is important to ask, "What does success look like?"

One way to ensure success is to ask the question above and then document the answer. Accountability is the cornerstone of success. It is nearly impossible to be successful unless you have a sense of purpose, which includes having a positive impact on others. Success does not exist in a vacuum. Successful leaders know that accomplishment comes from listening to and empowering others to be their best selves. Giving positivity to others professionally and personally exemplifies the confidence you have in yourself, and is a reflection of your success.

## Defining Success

When I first started coaching youth baseball in 1971, I worked with a recreational team in Manhattan, Kansas. I was given a list at the beginning of the summer of about a dozen ten- and eleven-year-old boys. Our job was to mold them into a "mean, lean, fighting machine," and have fun.

At 6:30 p.m., the first evening of our very first game of the summer, all the players were lined up in their uniforms in the city park. After hitting practice, I went to home plate to see who was going to bat first in the game. I was joined by the opposing coach and the umpire who was going to flip a coin. The umpire asked the other coach her choice, and she called heads. The coin went up in the air and came down heads, which meant it was her choice whether her team was going to bat first or not.

Most often in recreation ball, you wanted your team to go first, which was her choice. I went over to my team and assigned nine players to the field positions.

Before I'd had a chance to catch my breath, we were down 10 to nothing. When we finally got our third out, my team just stood in the field.

I ran out to the sideline and brought the team over in a huddle. I said, "Now gang, we're down 10 to nothing. I'll tell you what I'd like to have you do." Before I could explain further, one player said, "I know coach. I know what you want us to do. You want us to get them all back."

I responded, "No, I don't want you to get them all back. What I want you to do is think about what we did in batting practice. Each one of you hit the ball that I pitched. You were so good that my arm is so sore from throwing balls to you. I can't even lift it over my shoulder." I stood and waited for every single one of those team members to nod their heads, because they all knew that each one had been successful in batting practice and had hit the ball.

The other team's pitcher was on the mound throwing practice pitches. I said, "Look at Joey out there; he throws slower than I pitched in practice. You ought to be able to hit the balls he throws. All I want you to do is go out there and do what you did in practice: hit the ball and run really fast to first base. Try to score some runs. That's all I want you to do." Then we huddled up and broke with a big "Go!"

Each waited their turn at bat and sure enough, we hit the ball. We got on base, we had some success. We scored three runs that inning. After the final out, I got them all together again for another group meeting. I said, "Great job. You did it, you scored three runs." I turned to our pitcher Paul, who had given up those 10 runs, and said, "Paul you won't be pitching again.

Let's give someone else a chance to pitch." Then I turned to Ben. "Ben, what I want you to do is throw strikes." Those of you in the field, I want to make sure that each of you knows the ball is going to be hit, probably to you, so be ready for it. Let's try to hold them to no runs."

As they took their positions in the field, I got on one knee and said a little prayer. We were successful. The other team got a hit, but we got the third out. Our team came off the field and once again I called them into a huddle. "Great job! You held them to no runs." I looked up and said, "They still have Joey out there on the mound pitching. He pitched that first inning and you hit him, so you ought to be able to hit him again. Let's hit the ball like we did the first inning and we did in practice."

We broke the huddle with another big "Go," and they went to get their bats to get ready for their turn. That inning we scored five runs. Everyone was excited. Helmets and gloves flew into the air, parents in the stands high-fived each other at our success.

In that moment, I realized we were defining our success. We didn't let the score define what we wanted to do; we went one pitch at a time. We took a breath. We talked about our success and what was working for us and what else could work for us moving forward.

Now I'd like to end my story by telling you that we won the game. We didn't. We tied 10 to 10, which is commendable, especially from where we started at our first at bat in the first inning. We were able to make up the runs because as a team we put ourselves in a position to define our success.

Defining success goes beyond the moment. You define it for the situation you are in by listening to the voices inside you and pinpointing where you excel. You figure out what worked for you in the past and utilize that experience. Then you hold onto that success and apply it to future expectations put forth with real and authentic effort.

## Discipline is Key to Success

I spent three decades coaching competitive fastpitch softball in Manhattan, Kansas. The teams consisted of girls from ten to eighteen years old. My coaching responsibilities included teaching the fundamentals of softball, which included pitching, catching, throwing, hitting, and sportsmanship. The skills were necessary for us to participate in several major tournaments, as well as have a better understanding of sportsmanship and the fundamentals of softball. Having fun was also an important ingredient. Going to tournaments meant traveling and staying in hotels and taking responsibility for personal decisions beyond softball.

Going to tournaments took a lot of time, practice, and money—we made those investments. In order for us to benefit from the investments meant putting rules in place.

One rule I established when we stayed overnight was when we would all go to bed. This rule didn't mean when everyone would be in their rooms, but what time the players' heads would be on the pillow and there would be consequences if the rule was not followed, such as lost playing time.

We made it to our first tournament and won our first game. After celebrating, we went to the hotel. As a team we determined that 10:00 p.m. would be the "head on the pillow" time because we had a game at 9:00 a.m. the next morning.

That first evening, I was walking down the hallway and saw three young ladies, with their moms, out in the hallway, braiding their hair. It was five minutes past our agreed 10:00 p.m. curfew. I approached them and sent the players off to bed.

Since we had all agreed to consequences, the girls who were in the hallway did not play the next two days. This was difficult for the team because they were three of our best players. We did not play well that entire weekend.

Twenty years later, I attended the medical school graduation ceremony for one of those young ladies. Afterwards, we sat in a group. We spoke about school and the softball program from years ago. She said she wanted to share with me one of the most significant lessons she learned.

I sat there, waiting to hear about the skills she learned: bunting with a runner on first base, how to run a suicide, hit the cutoff, and how to hit with two strikes. But she did not mention any of those things.

She said, "The most important lesson was the time you caught me and my mom in the hallway at five minutes after ten o'clock, when I violated the 'head on pillow' rule you had made. For the first time, I felt the consequences for my actions. That set a standard for me through the rest of my middle school and high school years, and my time at the university. It's made me a better student, maybe a better human being, and it'll make me a better doctor."

Life lessons—they are important. It's not the rule, like "head on pillow," but realizing that the consequences of your actions make all the difference in the world in terms of leadership and being authentic and real.

## Nobody's Perfect

Nobody's perfect. We all make mistakes. What defines us is not the mistakes, but how we handle mistakes and disappointments in sincere, caring, and authentic ways.

Many fans believe that Michael Jordan is the greatest basketball player of all time. Truth is, he did not make it on to his ninth grade basketball team. He had to wait a whole year before he could tryout again as a sophomore. Can you imagine being the coach who cut Michael Jordan in high school?

Walt Disney was fired from his first job. The termination letter he received stated: "Walt, you're not creative enough to work with our company." Can you imagine the boss who accused Walt Disney of lacking imagination? On the back of that letter Disney sketched a stick figure that later became Mickey Mouse.

Even Oprah Winfrey had to overcome mistakes and disappointments. When she was fourteen years old she was pregnant, abused, and poor. Now, the singular name "Oprah" is seen as one of the most successful people in the world.

Mistakes happen. Disappointments occur. No one is perfect. It is not the situation, but how we respond and take ownership when we are the one who made the mistake, or caused the disappointment. If we respond by saying, "I'm sorry *if* I offended you." That is not an authentic apology. Make your apology as soon as possible, be specific about what you are apologizing about, be sincere and be authentic when you say, "I am sorry."

You want to make sure the person or group you are addressing knows you are going to strive not to repeat that mistake or offense. Be aware that what you do or say not only reflects back on you but on the group or organization that you are a part of, and you don't want them to carry that burden. You, the group, or organization is better than any single action—let others know that.

Everyone has bad days; everyone makes mistakes. It is not about being perfect, it is about owning our actions and behaviors. We need to make sure that others know how you sincerely feel about what happened. Apologies need to be authentic, which may require that we take some time to reflect on what happened. It is not the mistake that defines our character, it is our understanding of what happened and why and how we are going to make it right that defines who we are as a person.

It is okay to be vulnerable, and to recognize that we all have kinks in our armor. People will not judge us by our mistakes, but how we handle the disappointments we have caused. It requires putting ourselves in the other person's shoes so we can gain an understanding of why they are disappointed. Being defensive will not give us the opportunity to right a wrong, we must be real honest with ourselves and others.

Groups and institutions are also capable of making mistakes and causing disappointment. That is why it is important that all members are committed to being better. It is not enough for us to tout the fact that K-State, for example, is a great school. To live up to that claim, we must constantly evaluate ourselves and ask others, such as our students, our alumni, our faculty, staff, and supporters what we can do to be better. We then take that feedback to create training and other programs to respond to any concerns. When dealing with disappointments, human currency or grace earned must be taken into consideration.

Nobody is perfect, but everyone can be responsive. We can pay attention to others and be aware of those who have no voice but still deserve to have our attention. The best way to learn about our mistakes and disappointments is to pay attention and listen to others with authenticity.

## Legacy: What's Next

Authentic leaders demonstrate through their words, actions, and hopes a cautious optimism and a genuine interest in expressing appreciation for those who made a difference in their lives. Giving credit and recognizing those who made an impact establishes a legacy, which allows the good work to continue for generations to come. Legacy is the most meaningful characteristic of a sincere, caring and authentic leader.

To authentic leaders, the glass is always half-full. This positive energy is necessary to counteract the attitude of those who also believe the glass is half-empty or leaking and may never be full again.

Just about everyone who knows me knows that I have an optimistic point of view. Some say I have the "hopesies." I like that assessment. It is important to me to live in the legacy of wanting to do a little bit better each and every day. In my messages to others, I often talk about leaving room for dessert. I love desserts and

I often look at a restaurant menu dessert listing before I look at the main entrée. Now that I'm a little older, I have to be a little careful because my metabolism isn't what it used to be, but I still want to save room for dessert. It is an expectation of a joyous conclusion.

I think in terms of life expectations, meeting those expectations allows for a pause to celebrate or enjoy our accomplishments. My mom would simply remind me to "stop and smell the roses." That does not mean to overindulge; keeping things in moderation is necessary to meet expectations. Still, it is okay to enjoy what we find at the end of the rainbow.

Having a healthy outlook includes a sense of optimism. I probably got that sense of optimism from my dad. Although he had an eighth grade education, he was buried in purple; he loved K-State and was proud of my association with the school. When I was growing up, he always talked about his next job or the next opportunity. Among his many jobs, he owned a paint store. Actually, it was a very small room in a strip mall in Syracuse, New York. His small business was up against giants such as Walmart, Home Depot, and national hardware stores and paint stores. The name of his store was **Pat Bosco's Home Decorating Centers.** It was plural because he had a vision of eventually owning several home centers that sold paint. He always had a sense of optimism—the hopesies.

I remember one of our last conversations. Although we knew that he was terminally ill, he still had the idea of opening a chain of paint stores. He wanted us to go in halves. To glass half-empty people the idea would sound unrealistic, but to glass half-full people, it shows hope and the desire to continue to do something a little bit better. That was an attitude that he had. He was always dreaming of what was the next possibility.

You may not be able to control all of the circumstances in your life, but you can control your attitude by putting a smile on your face and in your voice. You cannot fake optimism, it has to come from within and be authentic. Optimism illustrates a sense of confidence, and conveys an interest in wanting to be accessible to others. Positive energy generates more positive energy—it's contagious. Enthusiasm means "in the spirit." The last four letters in the word I.A.S.M. stands for "I Am Sold Myself."

When you see the world as glass half-full, you think in terms of being accessible and approachable to others. Accessibility is the sign of an authentic leader. K-State president Jon Wefald exemplified that type of leadership. He had a can-do, positive attitude. If anyone tried to tell him that something couldn't be done, he set out to prove them wrong. That can-do attitude was contagious and motivated those around him into action.

At the beginning of his presidency, this transformational leader was told he should not spend time turning around football, or building a new library or art museum or increasing enrollment or endowments. Thank God, Dr. Wefald's can-do attitude prevailed and generations of K-Staters are and will continue for a very long time to enjoy these accomplishments and a lot more improvements at Kansas State University.

An optimistic point of view puts you on the path to success. Optimism gives you the ability to set reasonable goals and inspires others to join in the effort. A glass half-full attitude makes all the difference in the world.

## ABOUT THE AUTHOR

**DR. PAT J. BOSCO** is known to many as the ebullient face of Kansas State University in Manhattan, Kansas. For five decades he was the dean, waving to students from his window at Anderson Hall, stopping them in the Union to say hello.

In 2004, the Student Governing Association named the plaza outside the K-State Student Union in his honor. It was the only time in the school's history that a person still employed at K-State received such recognition.

Dr. Bosco has worked as Associate Vice President for Institutional Advancement/Dean of Students, Assistant Vice President for Educational and Student Services, Assistant Dean of Students, and Director of Student Activities.

As an associate professor in the College of Education, he has taught undergraduate and graduate classes in areas of higher educational administration, leadership, and volunteerism.

As Vice President for Student Life and Dean of Students, his responsibilities included: undergraduate admissions; new student services; student financial assistance, including scholarships; career services, academic coaching; housing and dining services;

LGBT Resource Center; the Student Union; K-State childcare; recreational services; the student health center; student organizations; registrar; parent and family programming; university counseling center; the campus food pantry; diversity programming; student crises services; and student-life fundraising. He has touched every aspect of student life at Kansas State University.

Dr. Bosco received his Bachelor of Science in Elementary Education from Kansas State University in 1971; a Master of Science in Educational Administration from K-State in 1973; and his Doctorate in Higher Education from the University of Nebraska in 1982. As an undergraduate, he was elected student body president and was the first student member of the faculty senate. He was a member of the Delta Sigma Phi fraternity and an Army ROTC distinguished military graduate commissioned as a $2^{nd}$ lieutenant.

During Dr. Bosco's tenure at K-State, enrollment grew to nearly 25,000 from 17,000, and the university broke records for freshman retention, graduation rates, job placement, and diversity. The university became the number one choice among Kansas high school seniors and remains so today. He is the only person in school history to serve on five presidents' cabinets, and as Dean of Students he has the longest tenure of any Big 12 University. He has served as an advisor to student organizations including the Student Governing Association and the Blue Key National Honor Society.

Dr. Bosco created one of the nation's first Centers for First Generation Students, and the K-State Parent and Family Association. He was one of three founders of the university's leadership studies program, which has become one of the largest and most distinguished programs of its kind in the nation. Each year, the Stanley School of Leadership Studies and Programs recognizes a graduating senior as the Pat J. Bosco Outstanding Student Leader.

As Executive Producer of the university's branding publications, Dr. Bosco was awarded multiple national CASE winners, including two NCAA 30-second spots and two recruiting videos as best in the nation.

Dr. Bosco is founder of the Center for Leadership Development, a not-for-profit consulting agency that provides training and educational programming to colleges and universities, corporations, and community groups. Since 1979, the center has presented the longest running student government leadership conference in the nation.

His community and professional involvement has included youth baseball and softball coaching where his teams won six state championships, president of Phi Delta Kappa educational fraternity, and member of the board of directors for Manhattan's United Way and Via Christi hospital.

Each year, the K-State women's basketball team presents the Pat J. Bosco outstanding student athlete award, and the university's Parent and Family Association has established a scholarship in his honor.

Among his other honors are being named a National Residence Hall Honorary member. He received the Acacia Frank Carlson Award; the Sigma Lambda Beta Exemplary Role Model Award; the Robert S. Krause ATΩ Outstanding Campus Leader Award; the K-State Student Union Vision Award; the 2000 Excellence in

Dedication Award from the Kansas City Alumni Club for his quarter century of administrative service to the university; and was inducted in to the Kansas State University ROTC Hall of Fame. He was named one of Manhattan Kansas' Most Admired People in 2004, and one of the Top 50 Kansans to know in 2016 by *Ingram's Magazine*. Dr. Bosco was named the American Fraternity Advisors Outstanding University Administrator in 2016 and in 2017; is the recipient of the Kansas State University football team's Outstanding Appreciation Award; the university's "Service to Students" Award; and two national Alumni Distinguished Service Awards from his fraternity, Delta Sigma Phi. The 2019 K-State Marching Band's Lifetime Legacy award and the Blue Key National Honor Society's Distinguished Service Award. Most recently he was awarded the 2020 Kansas Farm Bureau Friend of Agriculture Award given to individuals who have made significant contributions to KFB and/or agriculture.

Dr. Bosco's wife and children are all K-State graduates. Susan Bosco has four degrees from the university and is retired from the Manhattan school system as an elementary school teacher and media specialist. His son, Christopher, is a digital technology consultant, and his daughter, Mary Catherine, is Director of Strategy and Communications at Children's Mercy Hospital. Both live in Kansas City and married K-state graduates Stacy Dalton and Jonas Heinrich. Dr. Bosco has two grandchildren he describes as soon-to-be K-Staters: Henry, nine, and Hannah, seven.

## ACKNOWLEDGEMENTS

If you are reading this acknowledgment you have enough of an interest to learn that the proceeds for this book will support the Bosco Family Scholarship Fund at the KSU Foundation. Bosco Family Scholars are promising K-State students—most are the first in their family to attend any college and have demonstrated financial need...I am thankful to you for supporting our students and I am most appreciative for generous contributions of countless donors, including Mary Vanier—philanthropist, entrepreneur, loyal K-Stater, and a great friend to so many projects that ensure student success at the school we all love.

Authentic leaders believe, probably more than anything else, if they are to achieve any success, it is a direct result of those that support them. Mindy Reed is the editor of this book, founder of a publishing firm, and an accomplished author in her own right. Cindy Jeffries is a producer, director, marketing and communications specialist and producer of the *Boscology 101* podcasts. These two K-Staters are directly responsible for this project.

This book's heart and soul is the *Boscology 101* podcasts series, which came from my handwritten scribbles on yellow legal pads, speech outlines on small pieces of paper, and memories of personal stories I told to those kind enough to listen. There were no formal written papers, science-based research publications, or even articles from popular magazines to reference. Cindy and Mindy took what I had given them and in return provided me the chance to share some of my legacy with others. I am so appreciative to both for this wonderful opportunity they shared with me.

Special thanks to all those I served with, including so many caring and responsive Student Life Directors and staff.

In remembrance of Dr. Chester Peters who served as a mentor to so many, including Dr. Bernard Franklin. My friend Bernard will often call to discuss a student issue and ask, "What would Chet do?"

*Thanks to:*
Dr. Jon Wefald who had the confidence in me to delegate impactful assignments that helped move our school from great to significant. And other K-State Presidents: Dr. James McCain, Dr. Duane Acker, Dr. Kirk Schulz, General Richard Myers.

Coach Bill Snyder for providing countless examples of what it means to be an authentic leader.

Current and past student leaders dedicated to making our school better than when they first enrolled.

My Executive Assistants and the cadre of student office employees who always had my back.

Current and past Admissions Representatives who taught us what it means to crawl through broken glass for the school we all love.

Delta Sigma Phi Fraternity, the Manhattan Optimist Bullets, and the K-State Parents and Family Association

To all those who supported me and student success projects by their generous contributions, including:

Paul and Sandra Edgerley

Carl and Mary Ice

The Vanier Family

Rand and Patti Berney

Jim "Bob" Morris

John and Teresa Bilbrey

Richard E. Mistler and
The Mistler Family Foundation

To my We Are SGA family who gives voice for those who have none; my sister Kathy and her husband Tom for their support and encouragement.

I am so thankful for having the good sense to make the best authentic decision ever by asking Susan Ariola to marry me. Both of us first generation students who worked our way through school, raised two wonderful children, and now enjoy two grandchildren. In our final stages of our life together, I thank her for unconditional love, for being a wonderful wife, great mom, proud grandmother...and my best friend. I love you forever.

www.ingramcontent.com/pod-product-compliance
Lightning Source LLC
Chambersburg PA
CBHW070949080526
44587CB00015B/2237